A
NATURAL
STATE

A NATURAL STATE

STEPHEN HARRIGAN

★

TexasMonthlyPress

The essays in this book first appeared, some in a slightly different form, in Texas Monthly.

Texas Monthly Press
P.O. Box 1569
Austin, Texas 78767

A B C D E F G H

Library of Congress Cataloging-in-Publication Data

Harrigan, Stephen, 1948–
    A natural state.

    Collection of essays which first appeared in Texas Monthly magazine
    Contents: On the edge–The secret life of the beach–Life behind bars–[etc.]
    1. Harrigan, Stephen, 1948–   –Homes and haunts–Texas. 2. Texas–Description and travel. 3. Texas–Social life and customs. 4. Natural history–Texas.
5. Authors, American–20th century–Biography.
I. Title
PS3558.A626Z47 1988   814'.54   88-2149
ISBN 0-87719-107-7

Book design by D. J. Stout
Illustrations by Cathie Bleck

FOR ROSEMARY BERNEY

CONTENTS

PREFACE

WHEN I WAS SIX MY BROTHER AND I USED TO RIDE our bikes to a scummy little rainwater pond near our house in Abilene, Texas. The pond was full of old tires and cast-off two-by-fours with protruding nails. Tadpoles gathered in the shallow water near the banks, darting about in a witless frenzy.

Once, my brother, who was a year older, pointed toward a rotting piece of lumber afloat in the middle of the pond and told me there was a water moccasin on it. I'm not sure now if what I saw there was real or imagined; it seems to me that my child's experience of the world was formed as much by hallucination as by reality. The snake might not have been there at all, but I *remember* it, I see it to this day. It had a strange kind of shape, its body made up of a series of right-angle kinks like those of a stylized serpent on an Aztec temple. We threw rocks at it, but it didn't move. Its eyes were fixed on me, and the more rocks I threw at the snake the more those eyes seemed to hold me in some sort of terrible judgment. Finally its inanimate wrath broke through all my defenses, and I burst into panicked sobs.

I think of that moment as my introduction to nature. I don't know what nature is exactly—whether it is a category that includes human beings or shuts them out—but for me it has always contained that hint of eeriness, the sense that some vital information—common knowledge to all the universe—has been specifically withheld from me. Sometimes, as with the snake, this secrecy has seemed malevolent, but far more often it has been wonderfully tantalizing. For much of my life I have been obsessed with nature, but not in the way a naturalist would be obsessed with it—driven to classify, to define relationships, to comprehend the world's marvelous intricacy. I have simply wanted to feel more fully a part of that intricacy, to see something other than neutral scorn in the eyes of that half-imagined snake.

Reading these essays over again, I'm struck by how consistently that desire is expressed, how again and again their author seems to be pining for something beyond the range of his perception. I wrote these pieces over a period of eight years while on the staff of *Texas Monthly*, and I researched them in the manner of a journalist—through interviews with experts, background reading, and extensive travel. But I've never really felt like a journalist, and I think what drew me to these subjects was the opportunity they offered to hang up the phone and finally just go off somewhere by myself and look and think. While my colleagues at the magazine were working hard to make sense of modern Texas, I found myself drawn to those very things about the state that could never quite be articulated or understood. These essays are as much as anything a record of my own longing, of my search for those vibrant moments in which one can believe that one's existence belongs authentically to the world of nature.

Texas is an imperfect place in which to seek epiphanies about nature. It is a state that still takes pride in its continuing triumph over the land. I suppose I might rather have written about places radiant with uncorrupted natural beauty, where the beaches were not filled with trash and birds did not bathe in roadside oil slicks, where I could have imagined myself as the chronicler of a laboratory-pure wilderness. But I don't come from those places, and it seems to me that a city-bred Texan with an ambivalence about camping and an unsure way with a field guide can be a fair enough witness to a sullied and complicated natural heritage. The Texas landscape is not always beautiful, and in some places, at some moments, it is hardly bearable. But it is resonant and full of secrets, and this book is a tribute to the power with which those secrets are guarded.

WHATEVER INSIGHTS APPEAR IN THESE PAGES WERE gained on my *Texas Monthly* expense account, and for this I thank Michael Levy, the magazine's publisher, who created an institution that has meant far more to me over the years than a handy source for a per diem. Through *Texas Monthly* I have benefited from the counsel, and friendship, of a number of remarkable people. William Broyles, Jr., the magazine's founding editor, steered me onto several of the pieces contained in this book and provided much crucial guidance. Gregory Curtis, the present editor, has helped me sort out my concerns as a writer and has entrusted me with the latitude to pursue them. I consistently rely on the critical judgment of Lawrence Wright and Paul Burka, and over the years it took to produce this book I have accumulated debts to Nicholas Lemann, Dominique Browning, Joseph Nocera, Suzanne Winckler, Scott Lubeck, and Jean Andrews. The fact-checkers and copy editors of *Texas Monthly* have frequently saved me from embarrassment and have always pushed me toward higher standards of truth and syntax. Cynthia Hughes of the copy department gave this book a final check before lending her imprimatur, and art director D. J. Stout designed its overall appearance with a sensitivity and enthusiasm that is much appreciated.

Finally, thanks to all the people who appear in this book. They were unfailingly generous with their time and patient in the face of my ignorance.

Stephen Harrigan
February 1988

A
NATURAL
STATE

MORNING LIGHT

MORNING IS THE TIME OF DAY WHEN WE ARE LEAST receptive to the lessons of Copernicus. We may understand that our earth is a sphere revolving in the light of the sun, that it moves furiously through space neither forward nor backward, neither into nor out of time, with no apparent purpose and no fate other than entropy. But still a part of our intelligence greets each new day as if celestial mechanics had never been discovered, with a primitive confidence that the sun rises solely for us, to light our way and to warm our blood.

A good Texas morning may contain an unaccountable trace of melancholy, but I think it runs counter to human nature to face the rising sun and feel despair. Our most memorable mornings may have little to do with rousing atmospherical effects; they may be mute and cold, or sodden with stalled Gulf air. We might not even notice that day is coming, never glance at the gauzy whitish circle of the sun as it rises behind a wall of cloud. But we can sense the gathering confidence around us, the world's resolve to come into its fullest expression.

Let's say it is six a.m. From the sixty-fourth floor of the Transco Tower, the city of Houston is an endless field of individual lights—porch lights, bathroom lights, headlights—that shimmy in the heavy atmosphere. In the center of that field, monolithic and black as carbon, are the buildings of downtown. Not a single beam of light escapes from their windows, and there is no sunshine yet to give them any texture or relief. Along the horizon, running from south to north, is a thin flourish of cloud beginning to turn orange.

Already the cars are massing on the freeways, and from this height, in this meager light, they appear as a mysterious organic form. There is no question that an alien visitor would immediately identify the dominant life form on earth as the automobile, a creature of unfathomable motives and ceaseless energy, content to circle the dark, burned-out core of its city.

At the distant point where Richmond Avenue intersects the horizon, the sun comes up, seeping over the flat coastal prairie with a steady motion, bright as a welder's torch. It is a swift and simple event, unannounced by spectacular back-lit clouds or probing rivulets of light. The sun's plainness is beautiful.

As it rises, the sun seems not to cast its light but to hold it in, making the dawn so gradual as to be almost beyond notice. The glassy office buildings, which on another morning might flare dramatically in the rising and subsiding sunlight, merely pass soberly into day. Even when illuminated, Houston is still somnolent, still rich with strangeness, as the compact sun rides the horizon and the nearly full moon withdraws, losing its wattage and melding into the blue of the sky. Straight below, 64 stories down, is a billboard that in this transitional moment seems oddly provocative: "Coke Is It." Is it? If not, what is?

In the neighborhoods below, those people not asleep or already behind the wheel are rising from their beds and moving through their houses. Some of them possess a light-headed serenity, some lurch and stumble and wait for the tide of light to sweep them into awareness. One by one, they are turning off their porch lights, their bathroom lights, and soon the whole city seems to have shaken off its collective dream and regained its grasp.

Say it is the same morning, half an hour later. Six hundred miles to the west it is still dark. Standing on a peak in the Davis Mountains, an observer can look out onto a great volcanic plain and see no man-made light at all except for an occasional pair of headlights that cross the bare landscape like a moon rover. There is no wind, and no sound. Shooting stars are visible in the sky, and the moon has disappeared behind a ragged cloud. The landforms themselves—the products of ash fall and lava flow—are indistinct, just hazy shapes in the dark sump below.

Blocked by mountains, the sunrise never quite happens. The dark simply lifts, and the eastern sky turns radiant in its coloration. But the moment when morning occurs is as impossible to pinpoint as the moment when a soul leaves a dying body. Gradually the world seems less threatening, less solitary, less ancient. Birds begin to rustle in their nests, coyotes trot along the valley roads, and hawks soar above the fractured lava peaks, riding the day's first warm updrafts.

By this time it is morning all over the state, and even those who remain asleep can feel its effects. It is a light wash over their unconscious minds, a subtle reduction of urgency and detail in their dreams.

In a quiet Fort Worth neighborhood a mother has been up since five o'clock. It was her milk coming in that woke her, but when she walked into the baby's room to feed him, she found him still asleep, almost the first time since his birth that their bodies had been out of phase. Two months old, he lay there with his eyes clenched tight, his little fingers slowly fanning the air like the tentacles of a sea anemone. His blanket was trussed up about him just so. She wondered if he was dreaming. Did he even know enough of the world yet to construct a dream? She had read that at his age he was amorphous, a creature of sensation. He did not know himself to be distinct. She wanted to think it was her face he saw in his dreams – the emblem of his contentment, the rising sun of his scaled-down world.

Now it is an hour later and the baby has still not stirred. She might have gone back to bed, but she is used to the early morning by now, and this unexpected time to herself is a luxury she does not want to fritter away in sleep. She pours herself a bowl of cereal and thinks about garnishing it with sliced fruit, like the illustration on the box. Finally she decides against it—too much trouble and too much mess. The baby will surely wake up any minute. She can count on her two-year-old daughter to sleep till seven and on her husband's eyes to snap open exactly at seven-fifteen. As he does every morning, her husband will bound from the bed into the shower and be dressed in five minutes. He likes to be either asleep or awake and ready for action. In-between states make him nervous. He does not even own a bathrobe. She has never understood this—she loves to bask in her own drowsiness.

She watches television while she eats her cereal. A third-string local announcer is talking to a woman about a combination poor-boy art fair and fat stock show. He keeps nodding his head and muttering "uh-huh," all the while looking like he might suddenly reach over and strangle his guest just to relieve himself of his awful boredom.

After a few minutes of this she turns off the television and walks outside to see if the paper has come. The morning is hazy, and the dewy grass is cold beneath her bare feet. She picks up the paper and hurries back to the warmth of the sidewalk. Something holds her there, keeps her from turning back into the house. She is on the verge of some kind of thought; she can sense a vague opportunity forming for her in the still air. For that one second she feels as if she could slip into a trance.

But then the baby's crying distracts her. She goes

back into the house and picks him up, smelling his sour milk-breath, feeling her engorged breasts reacting to his outraged demands for nourishment. She walks outside to nurse him on the front porch, hoping to find that moment again. A large white dog walks briskly and purposefully down the center of the street, his head full of ideas. She can hear the sounds of garbage trucks, the yammering noise of some handyman's power saw, the raucous courtship call of a great-tailed grackle.

Then another sound: a mourning dove, its notes low and hollow and disturbingly evocative. It's a sound that reminds her of Girl Scout camp-outs, of early morning ground fog and bone-chilling cold and an odd, not unwelcome feeling of loneliness. Her baby lifts his head as if in response to the birdsong. Perhaps they are on the same frequency. Perhaps the sound, which is so tantalizing and ungraspable to her, meshes perfectly with his unformed intelligence. For a moment she envies her baby, because that is what she wants for herself: just to be here, just to be part of the morning.

ON THE EDGE

In the darkness, in the semi-wilderness, we tuned the radio to 1610 on the AM dial.

"*Bienvenidos,*" an unctuous male voice said, "and welcome to Big Bend National Park. We're glad you're here! Vast vistas and sweeping panoramas are just two of the things that make the park unique."

The voice was familiar. It sounded like the same guy who came over the car radio on the outskirts of Disney World, directing drivers to parking lots named for the Seven Dwarfs. Now here he was, filling us in on the park rules and accommodations. I turned the

radio off–I did not need to know where to hook up a
motor home–and looked out the window. The "vast
vistas and sweeping panoramas" were not visible at
night, but I thought I could feel the landscape open
and contract as we drove through it. Out in the darkness were great set pieces of geology–grabens and
lacoliths and cuestas–pure fundamental forms that
somehow made their presence known. A sign on the
side of the road pointed off to Dog Canyon, through
which Lieutenant William H. Echols had passed in
1859 with a train of 24 camels. The road itself followed the same route as the great Comanche War
Trail, a thoroughfare that had once been trampled into
definition a mile wide. We passed landmarks I could
not see but had read about–Green Gulch, Pulliam
Bluff, a mountain that supposedly formed the profile
of Alsate, the famous Apache chief who was betrayed
by the Mexicans and sold into slavery with his people.
All of this was invisible, all of it taken on faith.

The road planed upward, and my ears cleared
sharply, without effort. The truck's headlights caught
a small group of javelinas–dusky, spectral shapes that
made me think of tiny prehistoric horses. Several
miles later some creature a few inches long skittered
across the road.

"Pocket mouse," George Oliver muttered from the
back seat, almost to himself. He was sitting upright,
alert as an owl, his eyes fixed vigilantly on the road
ahead. He had been that way ever since we left
Austin, nine or ten hours earlier. He was looking for
dead animals on the highway, road kills that had not
yet been completely flattened, had not yet moldered

and seeped into the asphalt. There were, of course, lots of them: dogs and cats, deer, jackrabbits, porcupines, armadillos, skunks, mice, squirrels, and even great horned owls. Every few miles George would say, in his reserved, rather apologetic manner, "If, uh, it wouldn't be too much trouble, there's a pretty good hog-nosed skunk coming up here on the left," and O. C. Garza, who was driving the truck, would say with the elaborate courtesy one usually reserves for extreme cases, "Hey, no trouble at all. Can't pass up a good hog-nosed skunk."

Then the four of us would pile out of the car and stare down at a smushed pile of fur and bone and sun-blackened viscera. Sometimes the unfortunate creature's carcass would be too far gone and George would leave it, maybe taking its head along in a Ziploc bag for further study. More often he knelt to the task, taking out his forceps, searching the carcass for ectoparasites—lice, mites, ticks, and wingless parasitic flies—and then dropping them into vials of alcohol held by Linda Iverson, his unskittish associate.

George Oliver was a freelance zoologist who worked as a consultant for various state and federal conservation agencies. His main interests were reptiles and amphibians—herps, he called them—as well as birds and mammals. The ectos were a sideline, something he had fallen into. He sent the parasites to a colleague in Iowa for identification. The results of this research were sometimes published, with Oliver as junior author, in obscure entomological journals.

I knew George from another discipline. Some years ago, when I was editing a poetry magazine in Austin, he had appeared at my door one day with a group of remarkably accomplished and strangely moving poems studded with off-the-wall references to natural history, poems that took note of turtle plastrons and pikas and "the piss ritual of copulating porcupines." He looked much the same now as he had then. He still wore his straight brown hair below his shoulders, and in his field clothes—which included flat-bottomed work boots and an old straw cowboy hat that fit his head imperfectly—he managed to violate every precept of wilderness chic.

We kept climbing, heading up into the Chisos Mountains, the park's heartland. The Chisos are also known as the Ghost Mountains, for Alsate and others who are still supposed to haunt them, and for their basic demeanor. I was anxious for morning, so I could see them.

I was casually familiar with the region, having camped in the Chinati and Davis mountains and floated down the lower canyons of the Rio Grande in a canoe, but my efforts to visit the park itself had been consistently thwarted. Now I had made it—in January, at the height of the off-season, before the desert bloomed and the weather turned fair and the campgrounds and trails became congested with college students on spring break, with hard-core backpackers, and with the birders who come every spring and summer from all over the world to catch a glimpse of the Colima warbler, a rather ordinary bird that has the distinction of occurring almost nowhere else on earth.

DURING 1944, THE YEAR THE PARK OFFICIALLY

opened, there were 1,409 visitors. In recent years the
number has been edging up toward half a million. It
is a popular place, but it exudes a certain gravity that
makes it seem less an outdoor playland than a genuine
public trust. The people who have been there, or who
plan to go, or who simply take comfort in the fact that
it exists, speak of it reverently, longingly. For thousands of harried urban dwellers throughout the state it
is a recharge zone, someplace pure and resolute, an
imaginary ancestral home.

Such reactions to the Big Bend—the *despoblado*, as
the Spanish called it—are modern luxuries. For centuries it offered little but suffering and frustration. It was
a cursed, unfathomable desert country with a single
unnavigable river and a confusing welter of isolated
mountains formed from the broken linkage of the
Rockies and the Sierra del Carmens. It was a great
knurl in the landscape that obstructed the natural grain
of commerce and habitation.

The present boundaries of the park comprise about
11,000 square miles of this wilderness. The Big Bend
is formed by the Rio Grande, where it pivots suddenly
northward from its southeasterly course, cutting
through a series of magnificent and nearly unap-
proachable canyons. The river is the southern boundary of the park, which rests securely in the center
of its immense crook. On the United States side of
the Rio Grande is the northern expanse of the Chihuahuan Desert, whose dominance of the park is broken
by scattered freestanding mountains with names like
Mule Ear Peaks and Cow Heaven Mountains, and by
the high bastion of the Chisos range, which rises over

seven thousand feet above sea level. In the Chisos there are stands of Douglas fir, aspen, and ponderosa pine, stranded there when the lowlands turned to desert; and there are still black bear in the Chisos, too, as well as a shaky population of peregrine falcons.

None of these creatures appeared within the beam of our headlights. We saw another mouse or two and a flattened kangaroo rat that George did not feel was worth climbing out of the truck into the thirty-degree cold to inspect.

It took us almost an hour to drive from the park entrance to the Basin, which was five thousand feet up in the Chisos. The Basin is the place where most of the park's amenities are concentrated, a picturesque little aggregate of buildings—lodge, restaurant, store, ranger station, campground, and amphitheater. All of this was closed when we arrived. We could see little more than the glow of the Coke machines and a few lanterns alight in the campground. The campsites were rented on the honor system: one put $2 in an envelope, left the envelope in a receptacle, and then cruised around looking for a vacant site. At most other times of the year we would have had to reserve a site months in advance, but in the dead of winter there was plenty of room. We pulled up to a picnic table, unloaded the truck, and did our best to secure our tent stakes in the rocky ground. O.C. and I would be sleeping in my tent, a little green job about as water-repellent as cheesecloth. O.C.'s own tent offered better protection, but it was considerably heavier, and since we would be backpacking we had decided to leave it in the truck. Though he had doubts about the wisdom of this plan, O.C. remained unruffled. He was the perfect traveling companion: tireless, omnivorous, utterly adaptable to any social or climatic conditions. He did not grow moody or sulk, and did not seem to mind when other people did. He was built like a tree trunk, and in his bearded winter phase he looked compatible with the country, like one of Pancho Villa's soldiers decked out in hiking knickers.

Once both tents were up, we crawled into them, numb from the cold and from the all-day drive across half of Texas. The wind gusted all night, snapping the fabric taut and shaking droplets of condensation onto my forehead. I was reminded again of how my love of sleeping outdoors was merely a romantic illusion, that in fact I did not *sleep* outdoors, but rather lay on the ground waiting for morning, occasionally lapsing into a semiconscious state in which I moved about in my sleeping bag like an inchworm until I had found and settled upon the most uncomfortable portion of the immediate terrain.

O.C., of course, dropped off right away. He was a machine. I listened to his light snoring and checked my watch every hour. When it read 7:30 I unzipped the tent flap and drew it back to get my first look at the park. The scenery was extreme, what little of it was visible through the clouds. Then I realized that the clouds *were* the scenery; we were on their level. They moved through the Basin swiftly and gravely like a dense current, leaving little eddying pockets in the hollows and drainages of the mountains. The sun was not yet up, and the light in the Basin was cold and steely. The peaks themselves, revealed intermittently through the clouds, were monstrous and abrupt. They surrounded us completely, a perfect bowl except for one giant chink to the west, a natural drainage known as the Window. The Basin had begun as a great cyst, a dome of bedrock rising beneath the more recent deposits of volcanic ash and sandstone. Erosion undermined the softer rocks in the dome, collapsing the center and leaving a ring of mountains. Some of the mountains were smooth, having been eroded through to the original intrusive rock. Others, like Casa Grande, the most imposing fixture in the Basin, were dominated by blocks of lava that were reminiscent of the temples found on the summits of Central American pyramids.

George and Linda were awake, looking sadly at their tent, whose rear half had blown down during the night. Next to it stood a century plant, twelve feet high, each branch holding out its withered platelet of flowers. All about the camping area stood taut mountaineering tents from which people were beginning now to emerge, bleary and silent, walking to the full-service rest room trailing the untied laces of their hiking boots.

Despite the collapsed tent, Linda Iverson was in high spirits. She stood about braiding her blond hair and looking south to the highest elevation of the Chisos, where we were headed. She was 26, a native of Minnesota who had happened upon Austin and taken up residence there, working for a while as a waitress in a restaurant that specialized in omelets, and then enrolling in the university.

We spent the next few hours taking the tents down

and rearranging the loads in our backpacks. The sun finally made it over the mountain rim, and the essentially monochromatic winter landscape was subtly enhanced by its presence. The peaks ringing the Basin were just as imposing in the full sunlight as they had been when they were veiled in the clouds, but they were more accommodating to our perspective. They were closer than I had thought and not quite so sheer. I wondered how hard they would be to climb.

We ate breakfast at the restaurant and then browsed in the little gift shop. I bought a half-dozen polished rocks for my daughter and put them in a plastic coin purse that read Big Bend National Park. We made two more stops: at the park store, which featured racks of Harlequin Romances and freeze-dried food; and at the ranger station, where a genial, middle-aged volunteer park ranger in a yellow felt vest gave us a "backcountry permit" that looked like a luggage tag, and admonished us to carry plenty of water, since the springs were dry.

THE BACKCOUNTRY WE MEANT TO EXPLORE WAS known as the High Chisos Complex, a fourteen-mile loop along a well-maintained trail that would take us along the South Rim of the Chisos. It was a walk that could be made easily enough in a day by a casual hiker, or by a tourist riding up the trail in a train of sure-footed, sleepwalking horses, but we planned to take our time and spend as many as three or four days. Consequently, we were loaded down with water and food. We hoisted our packs in the Basin parking lot and ambled off to find the trail. There were roadrunners on the asphalt, pyrrhuloxia and house finches in yucca plants outside the lodge, and on the fringe of the Basin we saw six or seven mule deer, surprisingly heavy animals with ears the size of a donkey's.

The trail looped about pleasantly in the foothills for the first mile or so and then grew progressively steeper until it got down to business in a long series of switchbacks. The Basin dropped away all at once, as if it had been jettisoned, and every time I looked back I was astonished at how far we had risen. The mountains across the valley looked sheer, the vegetation sparse and grasping, but the slope we walked on was well-timbered with juniper cedar, piñon, and oak, plus an occasional madrone tree with its strange reddish-orange bark that looked like oxidized metal. I felt the weight of the water in my pack, which was scientifically designed to distribute its tonnage along some imaginary force field high above the shoulders. I secretly pined for my old Boy Scout Yucca pack, which was secured to a wooden frame with a diamond hitch, whose weight was felt directly and not as a vague, unaccountable sensation, as if some invisible beast were perching on the hiker's neck.

Every few yards George would crouch down and look off into the brush, at a brown towhee kicking through a pile of leaves, at a nondescript rodent he identified as a Texas antelope ground squirrel, at an acorn woodpecker. "Take a good look at his eye," he said. "There's something about that yellow ring around their eyes that makes them look insane."

We stopped more often as the trail got steeper. Looking down through binoculars I could see the Day-

Glo backpacks of a group far below us, but they were the only other people I had seen. We had come two or three miles, but I had given up trying to gauge the distance. I was merely relieved when the trail began to level out, passed over a saddle, and led to a broad mountain meadow carpeted with stipa grass. We walked past a pair of fiberglass outhouses and then veered off into the meadow and dropped our packs in a bower formed by the drooping branches of an alligator juniper. Then we took off our shoes and attended to our separate lunches. I watched with revulsion as O.C. opened a can labeled Potted Meat Food Product, spread the contents onto two pieces of rumpled white bread, and then proceeded to eat his sandwich with inexplicable pleasure. I opened a can of chicken spread, which was not much more appetizing, and ate a few dried apricots.

After lunch we set up our tents and then followed George around as he laid out a series of small aluminum live traps, baited with peanut butter and rolled oats. Trapping is of course rigidly controlled in the park, and collecting permits of any kind are hard to come by. George was, in his way, a fastidious ecologist. He trapped his animals alive, measured them, checked them for ectos, then released them in the same spot. He worried that this procedure might traumatize the creatures, a concern that would strike most conventional zoologists as eccentric, if not absurd. I had once watched a group of zoology graduate students at work in the field and had been appalled at the slaughter. They set out traps (brand name: Havahart), recovered the small mammals that entered them, injected them with sodium pentothal, eviscerated them, cleaned the carcasses with cornmeal, stuffed them with cotton, and arranged the resulting specimens in a laboratory tray with others of their kind.

"Most people are into this collecting syndrome," George said. "I've had people outright say that my data were no good, that there's no way you can get the proper identification from a live rat. These guys who go out and kill tend to be descriptive rather than interpretive biologists."

When the traps were baited and set, we made our way up the slope of Emory Peak, which loomed at the east end of the meadow and whose summit—at 7,835 feet—was the highest elevation in the park. There was a cave somewhere in the peak that George had heard about, the maternity colony for the Big Bend long-nosed bat. We worked our way up the steep slope of the mountain, above which sat the stark lava cap, jointed into long parallel blocks that had formed under the heating and cooling effects of Cenozoic weather. George found a group of snails under a dead agave plant, large round striped snails that he arranged on the palm of his hand and stood for a moment admiring. They were named *Humboltiana agavophila*, for the great German naturalist who had discovered them as well as for their affinity for agave composts.

George replaced the snails and we trudged upward again. The face of the cliff, when we arrived there, looked massive—there were no doubt dozens of caves in the seams of the rock. George set out and in a matter of minutes had found the cave entrance he was looking for, a high vault obscured by brush. Inside, the cave was dry and strikingly angular, made of smooth, collapsed boulders that fit together like masonry. There was a damp, ammonialike smell— guano. George squatted down under a low ceiling and motioned the rest of us forward, with his finger on his lips.

"I've found two hibernating Townsend's big-eared bats," he whispered, pointing to a furry clump on the ceiling. "I am going to attempt to get some parasites off them while they're still asleep."

It struck me as an ominous, eerie statement. "I am going to attempt to drive this stake through the vam- pire's heart while he is still asleep." I wasn't sure I wanted any part of it, but I watched, enthralled, as George reached up and plucked the two bats from their roost in one bare hand.

"Yeah," he whispered again, looking down almost tenderly at the bats. "They're hibernating all right. They're very cold. Feel them."

I knew that he had been inoculated against rabies. I reminded him that I had not. He said that the Town- send's big-eared was "not a bad rabies bat." I reluc- tantly poked one of the bats with the end of my finger —it was indeed cold—and then wiped the finger on my pants leg.

Linda crouched nearby, holding a vial for the para- sites. The bats were too drowsy to feel fear as George spread their wings and probed around with his for- ceps, occasionally blowing softly on the fur to expose a mite or a louse. The bats had very long, fibrous ears —like the feelers of a moth—that converged in the center of the face, creating an expression of alien wrath. When hibernating they ordinarily kept one ear retracted, but the more George handled them the more that ear began to rise. By and by the bats shook off sleep and grew active. One of them twisted his neck around, made a strange whining sound like a tiny disengaged motor, and bit George on the finger, which did not distress him in the least.

He was glad to discover two species of parasitic flies, which he held up for our inspection; they looked like pieces of grit caught in his forceps. A moment later he replaced the two bats on the ceiling as if he were hanging ornaments on a Christmas tree. Once their feet were securely rooted to an almost microscopic irregularity in the smooth rock, the bats flapped their wings once or twice, cloaked them around their bodies, and then, astonishingly, went back to sleep.

There were more bats farther back in the cave, which rose upward in a series of lofts to another entrance fifty or sixty feet above us. In some places a few square feet of roost accommodated dozens of bats, aroused now and watchful, with both ears extended. None of them were the long-nosed bats that George had held out a faint hope of seeing. He searched the cave floor for a skull or some other evidence of the species' presence, but when the light outside began to fail he had to give up the effort.

Back in the meadow I lay in the grass, exhausted, studying a hummingbird nest that had been constructed on an agarita branch. The nest was about the size of a plum, perfectly formed and covered with lichen that resembled a ceramic glaze. Up on Emory Peak the sunlight ebbed and flowed, playing across the surface of the rock.

EMORY WAS WILLIAM H. EMORY. HE HEADED THE 1852 U.S. Boundary Survey Team, which made one of the half-dozen forays by engineers and geologists into the Big Bend, attempting to establish roads and trade routes. The region was no more hospitable to them than it had been to the Spanish, who had tried for 250 years to secure their authority along the frontier of Nueva Vicayza. They sent *entrada* after *entrada* into the wilderness, searching for gold, souls, slaves, finally for lines of defense against the Apaches. The surveyors met with the same problems—a grave lack of food and water and constant threats from the Indians—and they suffered in the detached way of scientists, sketching their maps and tending their instruments while almost senseless with thirst.

It was the Indians who made the best use of the Big Bend. The Apaches were driven into the region by the Comanches, and the Comanches were in turn driven there by the Americans. Both tribes adapted, learning when the land could be depended upon to sustain life, when the springs were running and the *tinajas*, the waterholes worn into the bedrock, were full. The Mescalero Apaches traveled with their water stored in thirty-foot lengths of animal intestines that they entwined around their packhorses. They established *rancherías*—periodic campsites—here in the Chisos, in this very meadow. Every year in May, during what they called the Mexican moon, the Comanches would follow the war trail down from the high plains, raiding the Mexican villages on the other side of the river and living primarily on the spoils.

All of that carnage and enterprise seemed now to have faded away, absorbed into the rock. Over these very mountains had swarmed Chisos Indians, Apaches, Comanches, bandits from both sides of the border, prospectors, businessmen, scalp hunters, refugees, Texas Rangers, miners, Pancho Villa, and General Pershing. Now there was the occasional happy hiker.

Before dinner the four of us passed around a canteen and a squeeze bottle of biodegradable soap and washed the bat guano off our hands. On my little Svea stove we cooked freeze-dried Chili Mac and made hot chocolate with crunchy dehydrated marshmallows. After that, though it was early, there was little to do but go to sleep. It was very cold, and the sputtering gasoline stove neither warmed us nor drew us into conversation. When we turned off our flashlights the night was complete: there was nothing visible or audible in it. There was simply its presence, the same night that had presided over the Chisos since they had risen through the crust of the earth.

By eight o'clock the next morning the sun was way below Emory Peak, and the wild grass in the meadow was as cold as steel wool. The clouds moved across the peak in droves, or in fast, spritely shreds that reminded me of spirit forms.

In the middle of the field George Oliver was already at work, combing the fur of a yellow-nosed cotton rat with his forceps. "I'd like to find another flea," he was saying. "It'd be great to find another flea or a louse."

He discovered his flea after ten minutes of picking over the rodent and inserted it into the vial Linda held out. He let the rat go, watching for a moment as it scrambled through the grass to its burrow, and moved on to check the next trap, which was also full. "It's like opening presents on Christmas morning," he said.

Almost all of the traps were inhabited, either by yellow-nosed cotton rats or by harvest and white-ankled mice. George measured each one carefully, writing in his notebook the length of its tail and feet and body, and then checked it over for ectos. The rodents crouched and shivered in his grasp. Some bit him, and others sat still as he parted their fur with his breath.

George was delighted with the traps' success. He mentioned that his hands were numb from the cold, but otherwise he seemed happily preoccupied. He belonged here. His home in Austin was a minimal, transitory place, a rented house with a mattress on the floor and a few pieces of furniture that no one had bothered to haul to the dump. It was a *ranchería*, a foraging base.

I wandered about with my binoculars and watched a raucous group of sleek blue Mexican jays. I saw a woodpecker and a wren, some kind of wren. In my secret heart I knew I could barely tell one bird from another, or one tree or shrub or flower from another. I required constant tutoring; I needed a course in Remedial Basic Knowledge. Every trip I made into the wilderness seemed to subtract from my already meager store of information. I envied George Oliver his field identification skills—"Look! There's a white-throated swift. Its markings remind me of a killer whale"— because they were so obviously not just skills, but gifts.

I was restless. Even here, on the second day of a recreational camping trip, outfitted and made shame-lessly comfortable by a technology that would have stupefied one of those early explorers, I wanted to move on, to cover ground, to get it over with. I fingered the polished stones in my pocket, anxious to take them home. That was my problem: an absurd, pervasive homesickness. I knew I would have to keep one step ahead of this feeling, to outmaneuver and contain it. But to do so was a bother, and seemed out of keeping with the grandeur of this place that I wanted to love and in fact *did* love. I desperately wanted my emotions to be in pitch with the landscape.

DURING THE MORNING THE TEMPERATURE DROPPED steadily. We ate lunch in my tent, and afterward I broke into my store of Del Monte chocolate pudding, the one food item that experience had taught me was absolutely indispensable for packpacking. By the time we had gathered up our camp, slung it up on our backs, and headed out the trail for the South Rim, it was three o'clock. It must have been about thirty degrees, and it grew colder with every foot of altitude we gained.

We moved into the clouds, following a canyon where all the trees were covered with frost. Another mile or so after that the trail opened onto a plain where the grass had been worn down into the sod by hundreds of horseshoes and Vibram soles. A few hundred feet farther on, where the plain ended, was the most magnificent sight in Texas. The South Rim is a sheer lava bank that looks out upon what a casual observer might take to be a sizable portion of another planet. I walked up to the rim itself and felt a flourish of wind behind me trying to shove the surface area of my backpack forward as if it were a sail. I took a few steps back and studied the view. The Chisos, the high, self-contained bastion in the center of the park, dropped and then surged outward to meet the desert and a field of remarkable landforms. Far off in the haze was the Rio Grande, and I could see the other mountain groups—Punta de la Sierra, Chilicotal, that part of the Sierra del Carmens known as the Dead Horse Mountains—as clearly as on the three-dimensional model at park headquarters. The mountains presented a tableau of arrested motion, an everlasting instant of geological time. The ancient rocks rose and subsided like waves; they pulsed with light, and the light itself seemed generated by the power of the wind.

We walked on for another mile or so, following the rim, stopping every now and then to look out at the new perspectives it offered. We made camp in a little grove just off the trail. There was frost everywhere and the wind was intense. Little snowdrifts accumulated in the creases of our clothes. O.C. and I put up the tent, and then I tried without success to light the stove in the wind. I was sapped. We climbed into the tent and resolved to wait out the cold. I was wearing my long johns, several layers of clothing, and a bulky coat filled with some miracle synthetic; I was bundled up in my sleeping bag, which was rated to ten degrees above zero; and I was shivering uncontrollably. I had *never* been this cold. It was growing dark. We would be lying here with our teeth chattering for fourteen hours.

"You know," O.C. said, "I halfway think we ought to walk down tonight."

I had been halfway thinking the same thing. The

Basin was six and a half miles away, a long walk in the dark, but it was mostly downhill. In another few hours we could be sitting in a heated room in the lodge watching television. We considered it for a while and then pulled down the tent and wadded it up inside my backpack. George and Linda called out from their own tent that they were comfortable enough to wait the cold out, and would meet us in the Basin in a few days.

We got our blood circulating. The trail led out along the rim, then cut into Boot Canyon. It turned dark almost immediately, but we could see well enough with our flashlights to maintain a good pace. We followed the canyon down to Boot Spring, where there was an empty horse corral and ranger hut and a few picnic tables at which we sat and wolfed down some canned goods. Then we started off again, following the contour of the canyon, passing the Boot, a freestanding column of rock whose dark shape was strangely delineated against the night sky. Soon we came upon the steep, never-ending series of switchbacks that led back down to the Basin. We rambled down them, rarely speaking, overcome by monotony and fatigue. We could see the Basin far below us, a grouping of lights that never seemed to come nearer. It was one of those occasions when it was possible to lose all belief in progress, in time itself. I knew I would be walking down this hill forever, and when my feet finally did hit the asphalt I had the feeling I had simply appeared in the Basin in some ghostly form, that my real self was back up on the switchbacks, wandering in the void.

I lay on my back on a little swath of curbside greenery in the parking lot, looking up at the stars and removing pieces of ice from my beard. The lodge was full, so we drove to the campground and set up O.C.'s tent, an advanced apparatus that was supported by a cat's cradle of flexible aluminum poles and was as roomy inside as a pavilion. I lay down in profound weariness, as washed out, as eroded, as the landscape.

In the morning we hobbled up to the restaurant for pancakes. There were only a few people there: toothy, radiant young women in down vests and their ruddy, bearded companions, with whom they played footsie under the table in hiking boots that weighed five pounds apiece.

All at once the Basin seemed like a metropolis, alive with opportunity. I went into the store and looked at the cans of food displayed there, weirdly fascinated by everything I saw. To get our legs working again we climbed a small mountain, and in the afternoon we drove forty miles west to Santa Elena Canyon, descending all the way through desert, through the very scenery we had viewed from the South Rim. All along the way were strange formations, dikes and rills topped with freestanding rocks like the spine plates of a stegosaurus. There was an area quaintly identified as the "jumble of volcanoes," a place of low, bone-white hills strewn with nuggets of red volcanic rock that looked as if they had been unloaded there by a dump truck the day before.

Santa Elena Canyon is a deep gorge cut by the Rio Grande through the Mesa de Anguila, a corridor 1,500 feet high that simply stops in its tracks at the junction of the Rio Grande and Terlingua Creek. At this point the river makes a right-angle turn to the southwest, leaving a great floodplain on the American side.

The mouth of the canyon—with its concrete walkway and observation stanchions—is considered a must-see spot for visitors to the park, but in the middle of the winter few people were there. A hundred yards back into the canyon there was a stunning silence, or rather a stunning suggestion of silence, because I could hear a dim, thrumming sound, a constant tone that might have been a bird call echoing through the canyon or the operating sounds of some faraway piece of machinery. The whole thing was extraordinarily, soporifically peaceful. The river was as calm as the rock walls it reflected.

FOR THE NEXT SEVERAL DAYS WE HUNG AROUND the Basin, taking our meals there and driving back and forth through the park in the truck. It was as if, after a life of consequence and rigor, we had fallen into a decadent lethargy from which we could not escape. The food in the restaurant was consistently acceptable, and as we sat at our table, staring out the picture windows at the brute scenery, we came to recognize the other regulars. Most of them were retired couples wearing identical quilted jackets or vests with patches obtained at the other stops they had made on the national park circuit. They sat at their tables in comfortable silence, the wives with a look of loving forbearance, an air of humoring their husbands on this vast itinerary, this connect-the-dots odyssey of natural wonders. The windows of their motor homes were covered with decals – Yosemite, Royal Gorge, Mammoth Cave. There was no place for these big, lumbering vehicles in the prevailing backcountry ethic. Hikers came down from the mountains, their blood purified, their spiritual priorities in order, only to encounter the noxious fumes of a motor home. And yet there was something guileless and credible about these people; they were staking their last years of life on the notion that in these government-certified vistas there was something profoundly worth their attention.

One day we drove east, into a stark low-elevation desert sparsely covered with creosote bushes and agave and candelilla plants. Near the river we took a road that was little more than a jeep trail and followed it north until it deadended on the top of Cuesta Carlota, a low, regular ridge that put me in mind of an earthen dam. On the other side of the cuesta was Ernst Basin, a desert savannah bounded on the east by the Sierra del Carmens. The brush on the basin floor was thick, and there was a barely noticeable trail of greenery running through it.

We walked down on the other side of the ridge, following an unmaintained trail that frequently disappeared into the hard alkaline soil, marked only by occasional piles of rock. I was looking for a place I had read about in one of George Oliver's poems – "Syzygy at Ernst Tinaja."

M. A. Ernst had been a storekeeper and public official around the turn of the century at the little town of La Noria, a few miles north of here. He was ambushed one day as he rode home on his horse, shot in the back by parties unknown or at least never convicted of the crime. Later he was found leaning against a Spanish dagger plant, still alive and holding his intestines in place with one hand. He had written a note for his wife, who did not find it until just after he died: "Am shot . . . First shot hit, two more missed."

The trail snaked back into a deep canyon that cut through the cuesta to the basin. We followed it toward the desert and came across not one but a series of *tinajas,* swirling, polished depressions in the limestone that were all but dry. We stopped by the largest of them and watched the water bugs swimming in the few inches of water that remained. Compared with the outright grandeur of Santa Elena Canyon, it was nothing special, but the magic of place is an arbitrary phenomenon—I felt comfortable here, among the bleached, rococo rock forms. I would have liked to stay there all day, but the sun was going down and I was not sure we would be able to find the trail again in the darkness. Still, it was tempting. We were nearing the crepuscular hour, when javelinas would begin to snort and rise from their wallows, ready once more to face the desert gloaming.

That night George Oliver and Linda Iverson walked down from the South Rim and pitched their tent next to ours in the campground. They had had a good time, had climbed to the summit of Emory Peak and had experienced continued success with the traps. No sooner had the two of them touched ground in the Basin than they wanted out again, back into the solitude of the wilderness, back into their natural habitat. We ate some chili and then got into the truck and drove to the Grapevine Hills, a weird, haunted region composed of seemingly random piles of soft, scruffy rock. In the darkness we could see the haphazard silhouettes of the formations. It looked as if they would collapse at any moment, but they were obdurate and, to the fleeting perceptions of the creatures who beheld them, timeless.

For a moment I felt suddenly displaced, removed from the scene by a new wave of homesickness. It took more of my attention to combat it than I was willing to relinquish. I decided that one way around this intrusive emotion might be to think of Big Bend as home. I did. It worked immediately.

We stood on a bed of sand in the center of the canyon. We were the only people around for twenty miles.

"Maybe I can attract a predator," George Oliver said. He put the back of his hand up to his mouth and made a sound that he hoped approximated the cries of a small rodent in distress. It was a terrible, high-pitched wailing and squeaking sound. For a long time it had no effect, and George finally put his hand back in his pocket and turned to go.

"Wait!" Linda whispered. "I think I hear something."

The four of us stood still and listened. We could hear it faintly now, the sound of a predator moving toward us through the brush.

THE SECRET LIFE
OF THE BEACH

A WHITE-TAILED HAWK HAS SPENT THE NIGHT AT
the summit of a solitary live oak behind the dunes.
There is dew on the hawk's wings; he is sluggish and
cold. He turns around and around on the branch, positioning himself to catch the warmth of the sun rising
into a clear sky over the Gulf.

The tree on which the hawk sits bends elaborately
leeward. It stands at the center of the island in a
kind of valley, a deflation flat, between the stabilized
dunes near the beach and a bare active dune field that
backs up to the narrow lagoon separating the island
from the mainland.

The isolation of the tree suits the hawk. It gives him a sense of prominence, from which he derives a sense of security. Even at rest, uncommitted to anything except basking torpidly in the early morning sunlight, the hawk gives off an impression of awesome capability and utter indifference. He looks out over the grassland, blinking. His stolid body is clearly marked: a warm gray above, with rufous streaks on the wings, and a clean white underside and tail, which is traversed at the tip by a precise black band.

When the sun is a little higher, he begins his diurnal rounds, rising from the tree with a few powerful surges of his wings and almost immediately entering an updraft. The hawk artfully conforms to the movement of the warm air, letting it support him, adjusting the tension in his wings for direction and height. The same economy that guides his flight guides his will: there is neither wasted motion nor wasted thought. The hawk's mind is as clear as the air in which he flies. He scans the ground and notes without concern the high-packed burrows of pocket gophers, the scattered yellow flowers of beach morning glory, his own reflection in the water of a tidal pool. Far below him on the highway that runs the length of the island lies a dead mother possum, surrounded by the three embryonic forms that were knocked from her pouch when she was struck during the night by a car. The possum babies are pink, with black, skin-covered bulges of incipient eyes and well-developed forelimbs, which they had used to climb from their mother's vagina to her pouch, knowing the way by the trail of saliva she had deposited.

None of this concerns the hawk. It is movement that excites him. The sharpness of his vision, the expert trim of his body in the air—sensations that would produce a state of rapture if transferred to a human being—are part of the package of the hawk, instruments for locating snakes and rabbits and frogs. But within the range of his vision the narrow island is encompassed: it revolves around the steady axis of his perception. When the hawk flies north the open Gulf is at his right wing tip and the muddy lagoon at his left.

The island is little more than a mile wide and only a few hundred yards from the mainland. Though it is twenty miles long, its northern and southern boundaries are almost abstract landmarks, the sites of natural passes that barely interrupt the continuity of a long strip of offshore islands that shadows the Texas coast for some two hundred miles, from the Brazos to the Rio Grande. This island, like the others that make up the chain, is a barrier island, a sandbar that serves as a buffer between the turbulence of the open Gulf and the calm estuarine waters. Above its base of Pleistocene mud the island is an accumulation of sediment washed down from rivers, fanned along the coast by currents, and pounded into a semblance of geological form by the surf. The island's shoreface is paralleled by three submerged bars, with deep troughs between them, that are the last easily discernible features of the sea bottom before it planes out for its long, monotonous drop along the continental slope. The smooth, wind-generated waves of the ocean, coasting along the consistent upgrade of the bottom, trip over the outermost bar, regenerate somewhat in the trough, and then break and reform again for the next two series, finally reaching the shore itself with a weary, slouching motion. Because of the bars the surf is predictable but sloppy, the waves rebuilding and expending themselves all in a distance of a few hundred feet.

The beach itself is several hundred feet wide, and beyond it are the high and stable foredunes, secured by spartina grass and sea oats from the constant scouring of the wind. The grass flats behind the dunes are stable too, in their way, having been eroded down to ancient sand deposits whose surprisingly regular stratigraphy has been spoiled by the ceaseless disturbance of burrowing animals and rooting plants. But beyond this savannah the dunes are clean and virginal, expanses so utterly without shade or protection that practically no living thing interferes with their architectural purity. The dunes are lower than the foredunes, and blindingly white. And though constantly moving, they are not arbitrary forms. Their complex structure is implied by the wind ripples and slip faces that mark their surfaces. Beyond the dune field is a tidal flat, overgrown with marsh grass, that shelves with no particular demarcation into the lagoon and the deep mud that underlies it.

ALL THIS IS WITHIN THE FIELD OF THE HAWK'S EXquisite vision. High up in the sky the full moon is still visible, as pale as a cloud. At this time of the day the moon is simply a receding ornament, but its effects upon the creatures of the island are profound. All of the waters of the world fall a little toward the moon, as gravity demands. The oceans bulge outward, lagging in their momentum as the earth spins beneath, generating immense longitudinal waves that, when they reach land, are known as tides.

It is high tide now, on this island a visually unspectacular event, since the water rarely rises or falls more than a foot or two. The swash line—the farthest boundary of the surf—has advanced several yards up the beach, leaving a string of muddy, deflated foam and a new wave of detritus: broken shells, mangrove pods from the Yucatán, worm tubes, parts of crabs, plastic rings that once held six-packs of beer together, seaweed, light bulbs, gooseneck barnacles slowly dying of exposure on a piece of driftwood.

To the creatures that live within the surf zone the tide is a critical occurrence. Most of them live either beneath the sand or somehow secured to it and would be helpless if dislodged. They have no way of controlling themselves in the violence of the waves, no way to go in search of the tiny planktonic forms upon which their existence depends. The tides bring the plankton to them, and the creatures use whatever means they have for extracting it from the environment. Sand dollars, traveling just beneath the sand of the outermost trough, trap the plankton in minute spines that cover their sturdy, chambered bodies and move it along to their mouths. Nearly microscopic creatures called larvaceans construct a kind of house around their bodies, with which they trap and filter protein. Bivalves like the coquina clam open their shells just enough to send up a siphon to draw in the plankton.

In their makeshift burrows just inside the surf a

colony of coquinas is monitoring the violence of the waves above them. They can feel the power of the water, and the relative cessation of that power, by the intensity of the tremors it sends through the unstable sand in which they are buried. The clams read the disposition and duration of each wave. They hold themselves down in the sand by extending a powerful muscle, known as a foot, from their shells and then clenching it to give them purchase in the shifting sediment of the bottom.

A wave breaks above them, shaking the tiny clams in their burrows. They are aware of the calm of the receding wave, and they are impelled to reduce the tension in their feet and use the muscle instead to boost themselves up above the sand, where they extend their siphons and suck in the water, with its oxygen and nutrients.

Sometimes they miscalculate and rise out of the sand to find themselves fruitlessly siphoning the open air, having been stranded on the beach by low tide or an especially powerful outgoing wave. At such times the tiny, pastel-colored clams look like a handful of pebbles half-buried in the sand. But the illusion is momentary: the coquinas turn the sharp ends of their wing-shaped shells downward, extend their feet, and hitch themselves down into the security of the wet sand.

They are such dim, shapeless creatures within their shells; they are hardly imaginable, hardly recognizable as living beings. The shells are the calcified secretions of the clam, built layer by layer like the flowstone of a cave. The creatures themselves are as impalpable as the shells are exact: a blob containing viscera, gills, muscles that control digestion and motion, and muscles that hold the wings of the shell shut with remarkable tenacity to protect the helpless proto-plasm inside. The clam's brain consists of a few spe-cialized ganglia strung out along a neural cord. The creature has no eyes, no sense of smell, no hearing. Yet in some way it is as ardent about its existence as the bottle-nosed dolphin that has ridden the tide over the highest bar and is chasing a school of mullet now in the trough. Within the intertidal zone, as well as upon the island itself, there are no degrees of exis-tence, only a range of mysteries, secrets of perception that every species withholds from all others.

Coquina clams live for about a year if they do not fall victim to the wide range of predators that swarm or swim or walk within the surf. Bottom-feeding fish like drums or croakers cruise above the sand, probing with the barbels on their chins for buried mollusks and then popping the creatures into their mouths with impressive speed. Willet feed on the coquinas in the receding waves, grabbing the still-extended feet of the clams in their bills. With a twist of their heads, the birds then snap the adductor muscles that hold the shell together. Coquinas also fall prey to other mollusks, carnivorous snails that have the gift of locomotion.

One such creature is making its way now toward a colony of coquinas. It is a shark's eye, named for the center point in the whorled design of its shell. The shell rides on the back of the mollusk, which is an almost liquid mass of such volume that it is difficult to imagine how it could ever work itself back inside. Far in advance of the shell are the creature's tentacles, and below them, almost invisible, are two "eyes," blotches of sensitive pigment through which it can sense gross changes in the quality of light. The mollusk glides along on its foot, secreting a film of mucus to smooth the way. Its flesh is formless and almost transparent. The shark's eye burrows easily into the sand and comes out again, unimpeded by the underwater terrain. Though its tentacles are waving rhythmically ahead, more than just the sense of touch they provide guides the snail. It is drawn forward by the smell of the clams, a sense that comes to the snail through a minute organ near its gills.

It tracks the clams relentlessly and thoughtlessly, pulled along by its own appetite. The coquina that it will destroy is unaware of its presence and unequipped to escape anyway. Perhaps in the seawater it draws through its siphon the clam can detect the one-part-per-billion presence of the snail, but such an advance warning cannot mitigate its helplessness.

The snail closes in so slowly that its victim's death seems ordained, and the action itself monumental, as if the mollusks were two landmasses drifting together. When the snail finally reaches the clam it unhesitatingly smothers it with the mass of its body and begins the process of boring a hole through the shell, rasping in a circular motion with the minute denticles in its mouth. When the hole is drilled the snail inserts its proboscis and begins the process of absorbing the clam. It takes hours to accomplish this, and all the while the other members of the coquina colony pop up and down in accordance with the rhythm of the waves.

Strewn all along the beach are the empty shells of coquinas and cockles, each with a neat hole drilled through it. The evidence of predation and destruction is everywhere. The sea brings an astonishing variety of creatures, pulverized or whole and dying, onto the beach. A hardhead catfish washes up onto the sand, its sharp dorsal fin rising up and down with the heaving of its gills; a yellow sea whip, a thin rope of polyps uprooted from its anchoring place, ends up entwined on the beach with the tendrils of a Portuguese man-of-war; a small sprig of brown sargassum floats up on the tide, the host to a doomed and incredibly diverse community of hydroids, nudibranchs, crabs, shrimps, worms, and fish.

Perhaps nowhere else is the fact of death so obvious and unremitting. The most imposing feature of the seashore is the spectacle of life worn down and out, pummeled into its component parts. The dynamic of the littoral is a constant process of disintegration, a process evident even in the sand itself, whose grains are the result of the seemingly infinite weathering and grinding of rocks.

MOST OF THE ACTIVE LIFE OF THE BEACH IS HID-den, secreted away in burrows or calcified tubes, covered with sand, cemented to or tunneled into driftwood. The only consistently visible creatures on the shore are birds. Standing at the surf line, looking seaward with concentration, is a mixed population of laughing gulls and rather large, stocky terns—Caspian terns. The gulls are in their summer plumage, their heads hooded with black. The terns' heads are white, but with a black crest flattened back against their heads by the offshore wind. When they are not standing on shore the terns fly low and fast over the water, their wings canted sharply backward. They are diving birds, with the characteristic of dropping into the water as if they had been suddenly shot out of the sky. Whenever a tern manages to catch a fish in this fashion he must then defend it in an exhaustive aerial dispute with the gulls, who are more aggressive and persistent and are capable of running a tern almost to ground.

But standing together on the beach, the terns and gulls are at peace, narcotized by the rhythm of the surf. Sanderlings poke around near their feet, and just above the water a frigate bird soars, a strange dihedral kink in each wing and a quality of reserve in the manner in which it simply bends down and extracts a fish from the waves. There are black skimmers out there too, and spring migrants—swallows and Baltimore orioles and a chuck-will's-widow—that have flown all the way across the Gulf with instinctive reckoning and endurance.

Within the crowd of shorebirds there are occasional desultory episodes of mating. A male tern bobs his head, struts about, and hops onto a female's back, grabbing her by the neck and then flapping his wings and squawking. When it is over the male hops down and looks out to sea again, his fervor of a moment earlier completely forgotten.

It is the mating season for other vertebrate inhabitants of the island as well. Back behind the dunes a keeled earless lizard skims over the loose sand as lightly as a water bug. The lizard skitters forward for a few feet and then stops, bobbing his head in much the same way as the birds on the beach, advertising himself to whatever females may be around. The lizard is preoccupied with the urge to mate. His skin has broken out in black nuptial bars that run along either side of his body. Somewhere in the same dune field there is a female, but she is already gravid from an earlier encounter with this same male. She is, however, still flushed with her own mating display—an understated suffusion of yellows and oranges where the male has his black bands. Her body is swollen with the eggs she will soon deposit without ceremony into the sand.

The male lizard continues to bob his head, casting about in the vast dune field for another mate. Then he moves on, unfulfilled but undeterred, over the crest of a dune and out to a bed of hard sand where his long digits leave no tracks but where the prints of coyotes, foxes, and skunks are deeply impressed. Beneath a mat of vegetation at the edge of a clear expanse of dunes, the lizard stops, filled with the primal knowledge that to cross the barren sand would be suicidal. Overhead, the white-tailed hawk is circling, stable in the thermals, scanning the brush for a signal, for movement such as the lizard will give when he bobs his head in autonomic longing.

As the day wears on, the lizard becomes progressively less active, finding relief from the heat in the shade of the dune grass. During the afternoon most of the terrestrial inhabitants of the island are likewise holed up, waiting for the cycle of predation and opportunity that the coolness of the evening will bring about. The cycle continues, of course, in the ocean, and in the tidal marshes at the back of the island, where hermit crabs stagger about beneath the weight of the abandoned gastropod shells they have taken over, to which they have fitted themselves almost as firmly as the original inhabitants. The crabs are, for the most part, very small, their hind parts carefully contorted into the inner chambers of moon shells and whelks. Only their claws are visible, and with these claws they pull themselves along the mud bottom of the flat or up the sheer faces of rocks.

WHEN, AT LENGTH, THE SUN BEGINS TO GO DOWN, the hermit crabs are not aware of it, but to many other creatures the coolness and the beginning of darkness are signals to come out of their torpor and hiding and into their nocturnal wakefulness.

In the grasslands midway between the dunes and the mud flats there is a large, brackish pond and several acres of outlying marshland. In a red-winged blackbird's abandoned nest, slightly elevated in the vegetation beside the pond, a rice rat is nursing her five offspring. It is dark in the nest. The rat has reinforced it with bits of grasses and sedges and left a solitary side entrance that lets in some of the fading light. The babies are two days old, and already they are active and demanding. In only a few days they will be on their own, making exploratory trips from the nest and then, on the tenth or eleventh day of their lives, being booted out by their mother. The rat will then mate again and lose no time in driving away the male whose presence she has endured only for the sake of procreation. None of this, of course, does the rat plan. It simply happens, and for now she is wholeheartedly a mother, as devoted to the little squirming forms at her belly as it is in her power to be.

But the babies are draining her reserves of strength and she is hungry. Before they are quite finished she stands up on her whispery little feet and drops out of the door of the nest. She scoots around a miniature inlet of the pond and wanders for a while through the thick jungle of the marsh grass before returning to the shoreline. She finds an insect to eat, a small crab and a jackknife clam, and then, because she is so hungry from the nursing, feeds for a while on the partially decomposed carcass of a lizard. She works her way up and down the muddy fringes of the pond, and then her hunger drives her farther back into the vegetation than she would normally go. Suddenly, in some unspecific way, she is alarmed; she quivers for a fraction of a second, her heart seizes up, and then every muscle and nerve of her body come together in one great convulsive leap as a pair of fangs plow into the sand where a moment earlier she was standing.

The rat does not bother to follow the shoreline now. She splashes headlong into the water and submerges, holding her breath and swimming beneath the murky water. She careens off the shell of a turtle and, closer to shore, swims between the legs of a reddish egret. She makes it to the opening of her nest with an easy leap and lies inside on her belly, with her heart pounding and the baby rice rats trying to burrow down to her nipples.

The massasauga rattlesnake that put the rice rat

through such trauma is moving away from the marsh-land and into the drier grass flats. The failure with the rat has cost him no loss of momentum or determination. His passage over the loose sand is swift and rhythmic. He can see and hear and sense heat, and yet another sense originates in his tongue, which he sends out ahead of him to record the particulate density of prey in the air. This information is stored on the tongue and processed through an organ at the back of the mouth. The resulting knowledge comes to the snake as taste. Already now he is receiving an intimation, the subtlest bouquet of kangaroo rat. The sensation gets stronger, until it is accompanied by the thumping of the creature's feet, a noise that the snake hears through the ground. He positions himself in a coil just off the kangaroo rat's path. He is very still and trancelike. The massasauga is a small snake, and for a rattlesnake has a small mouth. But then his venom—a neurotoxin—is much stronger than most other rattlesnakes'.

When the kangaroo rat comes down the path the snake strikes him in mid-stride, injecting the venom and then removing the fangs before the rat has even had time to become aware of the danger. Once he has registered the fact that he has been struck the rat leaps high into the air and hops away at top speed. The massasauga does not follow or seem concerned. He simply stays where he is, gathering his body together in a loose coil, resting until some internal timer tells him that the poison has done its work.

For long minutes the snake does not stir, and then finally he begins crawling in the direction of the rat.

He moves his head from side to side, flicking his tongue and catching a strong taste of rat urine and fear. About a dozen yards down the path he finds the rat on the ground, convulsing. When the body is still the snake moves up to it, running his tongue along it and then slowly opening his jaws to take it in. But then the rat makes one last effort, leaping from the snake's mouth, landing a foot away, and then twitching until he is still again. This time the snake waits awhile before finally moving in to begin the process of swallowing the rat head first.

Back at the pond several dozen diamondback terrapins have risen to the surface, their heads stippling the smooth surface of the water. The heads appear disembodied, and in their fixed, identical expressions they have a hallucinatory quality, as if the mood expressed in those reptilian faces were the true disposition of the pond. The turtles secrete saltwater from their eyes, take in air through their nostrils, and bask indolently in the last remaining light of day. Soon they will swim over the bank and bury themselves in mud for the night.

At this late hour the pond and the surrounding marsh are congested with bird life: willet, avocets, Louisiana herons, black-necked stilts, American bitterns. They are all feeding, after their fashions, or stalking about, or simply standing still in the water, breathing in the calmness of twilight. Except for the bird cries and the sudden flights of blackbirds and terns across the pond, the marsh is mute and still, the blood of its creatures at low tide.

Now, as if entering a stage that has been set for

them, come two roseate spoonbills. They are soaring low above the marsh, banking and teetering and coasting in the invisible element of the air. Their pink plumage, deepened by the quality of the remaining light, is gorgeous and alien. The spoonbills cruise low over the shallow marsh water, ease down within a foot of each other, and begin feeding with their heads submerged, moving their odd, spatulate, primitive beaks through the mud. There is a strong but tranquil breeze rippling the surface of the water where they stand and ruffling their feathers. The burst of color they bring to the subtle camouflage shading of the marsh is startling; the color of the spoonbills seems a mistake, or a conscious provocation, or some sort of benevolent gift. Even after the sun has gone down the birds are charged, for a long moment, with its light.

In the darkness the massasauga moves across the highway, the kangaroo rat still an undigested bulge in the center of his body. The asphalt has retained heat and the rattlesnake pauses to absorb it. All at once he hears a monumental commotion from the substratum that actually shakes him a little from side to side. The snake's concern is uncomplicated and cold, but very real. He tries to get away but moves forward just exactly enough for a moving car to crush his head. Some moments later a solitary coyote, after checking the highway for headlights, walks out and picks the snake up in his teeth, then carries the carcass to the side of the road and eats it, heartened by the bonus of the kangaroo rat.

DARKNESS HAS COME OVER THE BEACH WITH LITtle transition. A cottontail rabbit moves about the shoreward face of the dunes, which is pocketed with the fresh burrows of ghost crabs. From one of these burrows a crab emerges, extending its reticulated limbs and wiping the sand from its eyes with its antennae. The crab needs to replenish the seawater it stores within its gills; it is short of breath. It moves across the sand and down to the swash line, positioning itself there for a low, spent wave from which it can extract the water it needs to survive its terrestrial life. Hundreds of other ghost crabs are doing the same thing, or foraging about near the surf for smaller crabs and for stranded coquina clams whose shells they can chip away with their claws.

Several of the crabs stop to feed on the long tendrils of a beached Portuguese man-of-war. There are other men-of-war in the surf, helpless to control their fate in the choppy waves. Beyond the outermost bar, however, is a large flotilla of these creatures, their purple sacs driven by the wind across the surface of the water. The men-of-war are not individual animals, they are strange aggregates of other organisms, all of them too highly specialized to exist on their own. Small fish swimming through the man-of-war's trailing tentacles are injected with a powerful toxin and then eaten by the countless solitary forms.

For all its biological divisiveness, the man-of-war's will is single. In some way it recognizes the danger to its existence from the prevailing wind and adjusts the puckered "sail" on the top of its gas-filled float to compensate, allowing itself to tack steadily seaward.

As the man-of-war fleet moves away from the beach

the tendrils trail across the form of a pilot whale dying of natural causes at the edge of the bar. Unlike the men-of-war, the whale brims with awareness, though he is old and emaciated and no longer alert to his dying. He has been drifting aimlessly for days, and the overpowering loneliness and fright he had felt earlier have been replaced by waves of delirium interrupted by lucid moments of resignation. The whale is twenty feet long, his deep black color unrelieved by markings of any kind. He can feel the breakers trying to lift his bulk over the bar, he can feel his bulbous forehead scraping on the broken shells in the sand bottom. The vertigo he feels brings with it a not entirely unpleasant suggestion of diffusion, and he sees his own death as a process of absorption by the sea.

A half-mile away the white-tailed hawk, perched in his tree, can make out the slick black form of the whale in the waves. He can see also the bioluminescence in each wave face, the collective glow of millions upon millions of protozoan forms. The hawk understands neither of these phenomena, but all that the hawk does not know is irrelevant. It is what he knows that counts. The same is true for the manta ray cruising outside the surf, for the mole tunneling beneath the dunes, for the beachcomber walking along the swash line. They know what they need from the island, and they sense that although the sea continually progrades and erodes it, its life is a greater constant than their own.

LIFE BEHIND BARS

WHEN HE MAKES HIS ROUNDS OF THE ZOO AT night, Dick Bonko often stops his electric cart in front of the primate house and sits there eavesdropping on the inhabitants. He says that the noise the primates make at night is very different from the madhouse racket—the shrieks and whoops and strange reverberant moans—with which they express themselves during the day. It is instead a low-pitched, mumbling sound, like human beings muttering nonsense syllables in their sleep. Long after dark, with only Bonko there to hear them, the monkeys speak in tongues.

One night I made the rounds with him. We sat in the cart and listened for a long time, but no sound at all came from the primate house, nor from the rest of the Houston Zoo. There was no moon that night, and it was so dark that I could not be sure if the movement inside the cages was something I really perceived or only imagined. I pictured all the zoo animals stretched out on the ground with their heads resting on their forelimbs, like bored, disconsolate dogs. They were sleeping, or merely waiting out the night, complying with their natural cycles in the constricted environment of the zoo. Few of them had ever seen the velds or kopjes or rain forests they had been designed to inhabit. They had no idea where on earth they were or what their presence here meant to the constant human swarm that passed by their cages every day. But it was impossible to imagine that all those animals—Asiatic bears and scimitar-horned oryx, tapir and tigers and fennec foxes—lay there unaware, empty of sensation, soulless. They knew something. What was it?

"Naw, they're not going to say anything," Bonko said, driving away from the primate house. He stopped at the alligator pond and cocked his head, listening again.

"Sometimes at night you'll hear 'em growlin'," he whispered. "They'll make a funny sound with their bodies—a vibration sound—and then that tail'll slap the water. You hear that sound and you don't know what it is but you're ready to leave the zoo. Then sometimes you'll see 'em bouncin' back and forth in the water. They get to quiverin', like, and that's when they give you the spook."

But the alligators did not oblige. They lay there by the pond, great flaccid shapes a shade lighter than the darkness around them. Bonko headed up to the reptile house, reminiscing along the way about the times when, making his nocturnal rounds, he'd been scared half to death by a stray house cat unexpectedly brushing up against his leg.

Bonko is the night watchman at the Houston Zoo. Like all employees there, he is a civil servant, since the zoo is fundamentally a municipal enterprise. He is a quiet old man who seems comfortable with his routine, which involves making a circuit of the zoo every two hours, checking on the temperature of the buildings and noting any obvious distress on the part of the animals. Occasionally he might have to roust a group of drunk medical students off the grounds, or put in an emergency call to the vet, or keep an escaped mental patient from nearby Ben Taub hospital from committing suicide in the bear pits.

Before he became a night watchman Bonko worked as a keeper in Houston and at a zoo in Clovis, New Mexico. Way before that, back in 1936, he worked on the National Bison range in Montana. "I don't know what decided me on this kind of work," he said. "I guess it was really decided for me before I even knew there was such a thing as a zoo. My dad was a cowboy and my mother's family were all stock raisers. I worked considerable with feedin' stock and my granddad gave me a Shetland pony when I was four or five. I grew up with animals. I have respect for them."

At the reptile house Bonko got out of the cart and went inside to read the thermostats. The lights were still on in the exhibits, and I could see the Houston

Zoo's famous display of the effects of a venomous snakebite—a model of a human arm covered with ghastly black sores that looked like some sort of carnivorous fungus. The snakes and monitor lizards and thick-bodied skinks—glistening and moving by patient degrees in their little dioramas—gave Bonko the creeps. He was more comfortable in the small-mammal house, where we went next. It contained a large assortment of furtive, dreamlike creatures: miniature lemurs that hopped about like crickets, tufted tamarins with faces like those plastic shrunken heads sold in joke shops, a flying fox bat that hung upside down and held her newborn against her breast with her wing.

We went back behind the displays, into a perimeter area where off-exhibit animals were kept in plain metal cages. In a little kitchen Bonko read the thermostat and noted the temperature on a clipboard. On the way out he stopped at the cage of a red-fronted lemur and let it play tug-of-war with his ball-point pen. The lemur moved about in a disturbingly human way, as if it were in reality a miniature man who had put on some weird, bug-eyed costume.

"I guess my favorite animals to work with when I was a keeper were the big cats," Bonko told me as we continued his rounds. "The cats aren't afraid of you—they'll come after you if they want to. It keeps you alert. You work with the other animals, you get lax. You don't stay as sharp in your mind as you do workin' with the big cats.

"I like the birds pretty well. If I was comin' in the gate lookin' for a job and knowin' what I know today about the zoo, the big cats would be the ones I'd ask for, and next would be the birds. I don't care about workin' monkeys at all. They're too dirty, for one thing. You never know when one of 'em's gonna hit you alongside the head with a load of crap."

THE HOUSTON ZOO, A MORE OR LESS TYPICAL BIG-city zoo, is in the process of evolving from a haphazard, exploitative menagerie to a center for wildlife husbandry. "We want to become producers, not consumers, of wildlife," John Werler told me. Werler is the zoo director. His office, in the reptile building, is not quite as large as the adjoining exhibit area for the endangered Houston toad.

We had a long, thoughtful conversation about zoos, during which the phone on Werler's desk rang with regularity. The calls were from people who wanted to know the zoo's operating hours or who wanted advice on such matters as inducing box turtles to mate. There was a call from a man who had acquired a Bengal tiger to supplement his ego and was now eager to sell the creature to the zoo. On April Fools' Day, Werler said, it is impossible to conduct any business on the phone. Secretaries all over town leave message slips on their bosses' desks advising them to call "Mr. Fox" or "Mr. Bear" at the zoo's phone number.

"We no longer want what we call a 'postage stamp' collection," Werler explained between phone calls. "We want fewer species and more-natural groupings of those that we have. This also gives us more of a genetic viability. Almost every major zoo is gearing up in this area."

Werler leaned forward as he talked, his elbows on his knees. He seemed to have a sense of mission, which is appropriate, since zoos today are likely the final hope for the survival of a great number of wild species.

Werler said he could not remember the last time the Houston Zoo had bought an animal. Most of the newer residents had either been born here or were on breeding loan from other zoos. The enlightened posture among zoo people these days is to regard the institution primarily as a way of holding endangered species in trust. While their wild counterparts are stripped of their habitat or poached into extinction, the zoo animals will be reproducing, keeping the species alive for the day when they might be reintroduced into a less rapacious world.

Everyone wants to believe this, but among even the most optimistic zoo people a secret, disturbing voice keeps whispering that the wild populations of the earth are doomed. Soon the zoos will be filled with living examples of creatures the planet can no longer support. There is already a term for them— "cage relics."

The Houston Zoo's progress toward its mission is impeded by the usual shortage of funds and by its own past, which lives on in the form of crowded and outmoded facilities. Houston's reptile and bird collections are among the finest in the country; it has a new if rather eccentric-looking gorilla habitat, as well as an aquarium and administration complex. But many of the zoo's animals continue to live out their lives in featureless kennels, left over from the days when the term "zoological garden" gave off no hint of irony, as if all those drooling, defecating, cage-crazy beasts were no more cognizant, or disturbing to their human observers, than an exhibition of exotic orchids.

I have from time to time thought of myself as being "against" zoos, but it is perhaps closer to the truth to say that I have always been troubled by my own fascination with them. The zoo was the nexus of my childhood. It was not only the animals that were on display there but also the possibility they suggested that all life did not disappear beyond the rim of human awareness. I thought of the animals as spirit guides, willing to point the way to this new dimension. I felt secure among them and managed to interpret their numbed awareness as some exotic concern for my own well-being.

But of course the zoo animals were not the benevolent totems I had invented for myself. They were misplaced creatures, kidnapped from their environments and displayed for human amusement and human profit. As an adult, I don't feel that connection I felt as a child. I remember only the polar bear, pacing in his stainless steel cage with a fluid, waltzlike motion that did not vary in the slightest particular for all the years of his life, or a gorilla—with that same metronomic regularity—endlessly regurgitating and eating his own vomit. Such behavior is not necessarily neurotic; it could be merely an extension of natural activities. But even viewing the best behaved animals in the zoo, one senses a loss, a kind of spoilage. It is a distressingly neutral feeling to stand there in front of a Malaysian binturong or an Indian elephant and realize that noth-

ing is happening, that no information is being trans-
mitted, that you are both bored.

But I keep visiting zoos; I am a "zoo-goer." It's a
habit, I suppose, and it has its provocative moments.
I came to the Houston Zoo thinking that if I was not
able to form a firm opinion about zoos, I could at least
learn something about what goes on inside them.

THE BASIC THING THAT GOES ON IN A ZOO IS WHAT
is referred to politely as "removing the fecal." During
a week at the zoo I heard it referred to politely only
once. There is a lot of the fecal around. Its raw materials are hay, fruit, vegetables, various sizes of dog biscuits, white mice, hard-boiled eggs, Zu-Preem protein
compound, insects, and—for the vampire bats—blood
from local slaughterhouses.

A young woman named Carmen Beard, a big-cat
keeper, was kneeling beside a small clump of grass in
the tiger pit. It was evident that one of the tigers had
taken his ease at this spot a few days back. Beard
picked through the grass with a look of professional
distaste and then, seeing that it was beyond salvation,
simply uprooted it and tossed it into her garbage bag.

The tiger habitat consists of an island surrounded by
a deep dry moat, the whole thing made out of some
sort of spray-on concrete that is meant to suggest solid
rock but feels brittle and hollow beneath the feet.
While I glanced back across the moat to be sure the
tigers were still locked up in their holding pens, Beard
traipsed across the island and then down into the moat
carrying her shovel and trash bag. She sang a John
Denver song to herself as she shoveled the scat.

"What gets me," she said, interrupting her song, "is you'll be in this pit cleaning it out and the people will just stand up there and stare at you. I don't know why they're so fascinated. Do they think these animals clean up after themselves?

"I was talking to these people the other night. When I told them where I worked, this girl says, 'Can you believe that? She has to shovel lion shit and she *likes* it!' Well, I don't like that part of it, but it's not that big a deal. It's like having a child and having to change its diaper."

Down in the moat her voice bounced off the textured walls. "I'm not real wild about this moat at all," she said. "It's beautiful and everything, but it only has this one tiny drain. Those cats they put in here have got really big feces that just won't go down that drain. Then there's this echo. When there are a lot of kids up there screaming it sounds like an insane asylum. It's really eerie. I can imagine how those poor cats must feel."

After she was through with the moat Beard walked back inside the building. The interior of the cat house consists of a wide corridor with cages on both sides, each one of which has an outside compartment that serves as the display area. I had been advised to walk in the center of the corridor, since the cats have been known to take swipes at passersby. At this time of the morning—eight o'clock, an hour before the zoo opens to the public—they were alert and curious. I was aware of their eyes, which were as hard and brilliant as minerals, and of their languid, soaring grace when they jumped up and down off their wooden platforms. The tigers and lions and leopards tracked me with their eyes as I walked down the hallway, and their keen scrutiny made me realize that I was no longer in the zoo; I was in their home.

"Albert!" Beard called to one of the Bengal tigers, who had laid his great head up against the bars and was staring off into space in a masterful feline way. "That's my boy! You're my favorite kitty, yes, you are!"

Beard is a slight woman in her early twenties, with a forthright mammalian love for the great cats and bears that are in her charge. The way she spoke to the tigers and scratched their big tabby ears made me think she saw herself as their defender; someone who, if the battle lines were ever drawn, would stand on the side of the animals.

She started out working in the children's zoo, but after her husband died she didn't feel like meeting and dealing with the public every day. She wanted quiet and privacy, the mute solace of pacing beasts. The management assigned her to the bears and cats. It's the most dangerous job in the zoo, since it is assumed that a Kodiak bear or a Bengal tiger would not think twice about eating its beloved keeper if it should find itself suddenly in the same pit with her.

While I stood in the center of the corridor and stared at the cats, Beard and another woman keeper, Pat O'Conner, hosed out the interior cages, every once in a while giving the occupants a friendly squirt.

"Are zoos good or are zoos bad?" O'Conner mused as she yanked a kink out of her hose. "I don't know. You can weigh the pros and cons forever; it's like a balance scale. All of us sit around and talk about zoos all the time, trying to decide."

As the cats slunk and leaped all about them and growled for their Zu-Preem, the two women showed me snapshots of a snow leopard cub that had been born in the zoo in the spring and had died at the age of ten weeks from causes that were still undetermined. They commented on the photographs in a wistful, detached manner. Since the snow leopard is an endangered species, the cub's body had been donated to the Houston Museum of Natural Science instead of being hauled to the dump, which is where mosts of the animals that die at the zoo go.

"They're going to mount him," Beard said. "I'm going to go over there when they're through, I guess. I know it's going to upset me, but I just want to know if they did a good job."

I SPENT SOME TIME IN THE BIRD AREA, ADMIRING the zoo's collection of Central and South American guans and curassows, which are varieties of wild ornamental fowl, wattled and tufted, with radiant plumage. Certain species of guans, I had read in my animal encyclopedia, are "irresistibly attracted to fire" and are lured to their capture by small fires set in the branches of trees.

The guans and curassows were all housed in a string of outdoor cages known as the pheasant run. This was a specialized collection with only one anomaly, an apparition called the great hornbill. The hornbill's beak, like the toucan's, looks like an oversized wax banana, but the beak has an extra component above it, a kind of air scoop that makes the entire bird look—as we used to say of eccentric otherworldly automobiles—"customized."

The bird house itself was closed to the public because of an outbreak of Newcastle disease in the city. The curator, Robert Berry, took me through anyway. It's an intriguing building, with large exhibit windows and an open "rain forest" where the birds fly about more or less freely.

Berry is a dry, unsentimental man who put himself through college working as a professional dancer. Before he came to work at the zoo he was a private aviculturist. "I don't have any emotional attachment to birds at all," he said as we stood in the rain forest. "I respect them as living creatures, but I don't like to scratch them on the head and all that. I appreciate the beauty and the behavior of them."

Berry earned international attention for the Houston Zoo when he bred, for the first time in captivity, a scarlet cock-of-the-rock chick. Cocks-of-the-rock come from the Amazon valley and have huge puffball crests on their heads that make the males, with their bright orange plumage, look like pieces of fruit.

After the first chick was born Berry and his associates fretted about its diet until they discovered that the benign-looking cock-of-the-rock was in fact a latent bird of prey. The mother passed up the fruit she was offered in favor of a mouse that she caught herself. The keepers, who had been setting out rodent poison, took the mouse away from her, but then Berry brought a lizard from the reptile house and held it up in the air. The female immediately swooped down from her perch, plucked the lizard out of Berry's fingers, crushed it in her beak, and poked it down the chick's throat.

Although the chick died soon after this break-through, two more were born the next year. Berry took them home with him, nursing them 24 hours a day for six weeks, peeling their grapes for them, feeding them chopped newborn mice and blueberries, and monitoring—as Berry wrote in an article for a zoo magazine—"the character of the bowels." One of the birds died; the other, named Geronimo, survived, although Berry had a few tense moments in transporting him to the zoo. "The bird became carsick and regurgitated all of its food," he wrote. "Not only did I go into shock, I also became suicidal."

On my way out of the building I stopped for a while at the exhibit featuring a male cock-of-the-rock. The bird sat on a limb, placid and undemanding. It and the rest of the birds elicited curiosity and occasional amazement, but one could view them without that emotional disturbance that the more sentient and slovenly creatures of the zoo provoke.

THE BIRDS ARE LIVING ORNAMENTS, ELEMENTS IN A design, but there are some animals that no human design can truly accommodate. I went into the primate house, pausing to dip the soles of my shoes into a chemical bath so that I would not track in the diseases of the outside world. Inside, the primate house had the red brick construction and wide corridors of an elementary school. One of the keepers was eating a slice of lemon pie for breakfast, and another was heating a frozen sweet roll on a piece of aluminum foil that was placed on the burner of a stove.

The siamang gibbons had started their morning hooting, and it was difficult to hear anyone speak. The gibbons had a big cage at one end of the house, and as they yelled they swung about on their grapevines, moving through the air with an astonishing, fluid velocity. In the wild they are capable of grabbing birds in flight.

I strolled down the corridor with an old-time keeper named Oscar Mendieta. He was rubbing with a rag at a dark spot on his shirt where a chimpanzee named Kamaka had just scored a hit with his own byproducts. "In the morning he'll throw carrots or biscuits at me," Mendieta said, sounding hurt, "but shit he seldom throws anymore."

When we passed Kamaka's cage the chimpanzee beat furiously against the walls and bared his fangs but threw nothing. An agile gibbon across the hall casually shoved her posterior up against the bars. "She's in estrus right now," Mendieta said. "She's presenting to me. She always does that."

Mendieta said he had been at the zoo since 1957. Today the Houston Zoo requires of its employees some sort of formal animal care experience, which can be acquired by a kind of apprenticeship set up through the children's zoo. But in 1957 there were no particular qualifications. Mendieta had been working for an oil drum company, washing out barrels. One day he and his wife visited the zoo. "You know what, honey?" he said. "I think I'd like to work here." He took the city civil service test and found there were openings in water, sewer, and zoo.

"When I retire I plan to raise chickens or something," he told me. "I don't think I can ever get away from working with animals."

For most of the morning the staff cleaned out the cages and washed the floors with a chemical solution. I watched as Beryl Fisher, a former circus elephant trainer, entered the orangutan cage carrying two grocery bags filled with Purina Monkey Chow and fruit. The orangs liked to open the bags themselves and compare the contents.

While Fisher sat in the center of the cage they soared overhead on the grapevines and dropped, unannounced, into her lap. Then they stalked about on the sides of their feet with their arms wrapped about their torsos, staring at me through the bars. I could not help reading the gazes of the other primates as sober and accusing, but the orangutans emanated an unsettling mildness. These two had been born and bred in zoos, but in the forests of Borneo and Sumatra, where their species is being harassed into extinction, the word "orangutan" suggests a shadowy human nature — it means "man of the woods."

THE HOUSTON ZOO HAS ONE GORILLA. IT USED TO have two, but now a sign at the entrance of the habitat informs visitors: "Due to the untimely death of 'Je-Je,' our male gorilla, from colitis with secondary kidney failure, only the female is on display."

The female's name is Vanilla. She lives by herself in a large circular building that looks from the outside like the stump of a giant tree. The exhibit area is contained indoors, a great swath of stage scenery with sculptured terraces and dead trees and a tiny waterfall that cascades through a series of pools. Off the exhibit area are small cages where Vanilla prefers to spend her time. When the keeper leaves in the afternoon he turns on a television and Vanilla takes her food into one of these cages and watches cartoons.

When I dropped by one morning Bill Grissom, Vanilla's keeper, had locked her out in the exhibit area and was waiting for her to urinate so he could get a sample of her urine and run it through the contents of a box labeled "Subhuman Primate Pregnancy Test." In great apes, the test works not only for discovering pregnancy but for determining ovulation. Once they had Vanilla's ovulation pattern figured out, they'd try to inseminate her.

"The problem is the males," Grissom told me. "A guy at Baylor has electroejaculated five different gorillas and they've all been infertile."

Grissom let Vanilla in and gave her a cup of orange juice, milk, and wheat-germ oil mixture, along with a raw egg. She cracked the egg in one hand and sucked out the contents, then looked at me and stuck her tongue out.

"That's a greeting," Grissom said. "She expects you to return it."

I did, but it seemed to communicate nothing to her. She held out her hand, wanting me to touch it. I had been warned not to, since one or the other of us could transmit TB. I just looked at the hand, feeling uncertain and flustered. The nails were black and very thick, and the palm and fingers looked upholstered. She kept withdrawing her hand and offering it again distractedly, as if it was a matter of indifference to her whether I touched it or not.

"Sometimes she's just like us," Grissom said. "She gets off in her own little world. Since Je-Je died she's kind of a crybaby at times. When I leave her out in the morning to pee she'll scream at me, like she's saying, 'Come back! Don't leave me out here!'

"Je-Je was probably the biggest draw of the whole zoo. Sometimes you try to forget about him, but the public won't let you. They come in and say they remember how he used to do something or other and it'll bring it all back."

Grissom lives in fear that Vanilla will contract TB or some other disease from the visitors. He or another keeper usually sits on a folding chair out in front of the habitat, to make sure no one throws anything inside it. Vanilla can see him out there while she is on display; in that constant stream of twittering, gaping, guffawing creatures about whom she knows nothing, there is at least one steady, familiar face.

DURING MOST OF MY TIME AT THE ZOO I WAS PART of that crowd, drifting along with them from cage to habitat in an aimless fashion, roving past a whole section of animals and barely seeing them at all. I kept making the same circuit of the zoo over and over, pacing, wanting to cover ground. Eventually certain animals began to stand out. In the children's zoo I watched a group of alligator snapping turtles through a window in the side of their pool. They lay on the bottom, and every now and then a single perfect bubble would emerge from one of their bony nostrils.

They had pale, parchment-colored eyes overlaid with a design that reminded me of an old-fashioned television test pattern. When it was time for them to come up for air they had to fight their way off the bottom, clawing for the surface in a heavy, ungainly manner.

In that same part of the zoo there were two Galápagos tortoises mating, the male propped up against the female's back as if some fortuitous natural event like an earthquake had placed him there. He made a deep lowing noise with each thrust and moved against her back like a jeep stuck in high gear at the bottom of a hill.

Early in the morning, before the Houston miasma had had a chance to assert itself and cause the animals to wheeze and pant and lollygag around, before the smell of stale popcorn began to infest the air, it was possible to believe that the zoo was an innocent pleasure. That was when you would see Kodiak bears, as large as bison, perform backward somersaults; when the keepers led skittish camels around the grounds for their morning walk. At that hour the most mysterious, compelling animals in the zoo turned out to be the antelope and deer I routinely passed by, giving them hardly a look as I trailed my fingers along their chain-link corrals. Every movement of the small fallow deer seemed involuntary, hinged on some ancient evolutionary lesson. But the great horse-headed antelopes, the nylghais, the nyalas, were more aware of themselves. Their bodies were disjointed and misproportioned; they seemed to have turned out that way not in fulfillment of the genetic code but by an act of will on the part of the animal.

In the reptile house every creature had that air of deliberate presence, of having been created for a reason that human beings were somehow specifically proscribed from understanding.

In the hallways and warrens behind the exhibit cages, the reptile keepers, who as a rule were bearded and cerebral, spent a good deal of time cleaning the glass in terrariums, transferring torpid snakes from one to the other as if they were coils of stout wire.

"Mosts of the animals back here," a keeper named John McLain told me, "are juveniles being raised to maturity or separated for breeding purposes. This one, for instance, is a male, and this one over here is a female. When they finally meet each other we hope there'll be more than a handshake going on."

The snakes he was referring to were Bismarck ringed pythons. There were other pythons around: Angolans, reticulateds (which the staff called retics), and a baby green tree python, which was brilliant yellow in its immaturity and, when coiled upon a twig, managed to suggest a sea horse.

Placed at intervals throughout the reptile house were wall units labeled "Snakebite Alarm Box." If a keeper should get bitten by a venomous snake—an event that has not happened here for years—the alarm is sounded in the reptile house. The zoo keeps antivenin on hand—"If we can't get the antivenin," McLain said, "we won't stock the snake"—and has frequent snakebite drills to keep reaction time to a minimum.

While McLain cleaned the terrariums I wandered about a little, inspecting various exotic tree frogs, a washtub full of three-week-old Chinese alligators, a pair of deadly gaboon vipers as thick as my arm that made a loud snorting sound I could hear twenty yards away. There was another noise, an incessant squeaking that I realized I had been hearing all along. It came from a small cage full of newborn mice, pink and hairless, crowded together like packing material. There was another cage next to it, equally crowded with baby mice in the next stage of development, with new pelts of white fur.

I could not take my eyes off them. All those mewling infant mice, as insignificant as the sawdust that covered the bottoms of the cages in which they would be ingested by a finicky snake. They reminded me of the term used by fishermen to describe the unwelcome, inedible species that occasionally take the hook: "trash fish."

FROM THE REPTILE HOUSE IT WAS PERHAPS FIFTY yards and several rungs up the evolutionary ladder to the elephant compound. The keeper there is a woman named Lucille Sweeney, and when I walked up she was putting her two Indian elephants through a low-key circus routine that involved having them stand up on a stool and raise their forelimbs. Sweeney works the elephants this way not to please the visitors but to keep the elephants in control and used to her presence. That way she can groom them with no trouble, scraping off dead skin with a stiff wire brush and maintaining their feet, which are subject to a variety of diseases.

When the male elephant–Thai–reared up on the

stool, he used the opportunity to unload a prodigious amount of the fecal. There was a first-grade class there watching him, and they were properly grossed out and agog at the evidence of his subsequent sexual arousal. The teachers tried to divert the kids' attention to Indu, the female, who was considerably more discreet.

"Get that trunk up, Indu," Sweeney was calling. "Get it up. Oh, look at that girl stand."

Lucille Sweeney first came to work at the zoo more than ten years ago after she had finished her honors thesis on William Faulkner. She thought she would give herself a year to "get animals out of my system," but it became her life's work.

"The first elephant I ever saw was at the circus. They let us little ones come up close and sit on the floor. So there I was, watching these huge animals go by. I was awestruck. That these creatures would actually work for a human being when they had so much power to hurt was beautiful to me."

She used to visit the Houston Zoo a lot when she was a little girl. Her favorite animal was the bull elephant, Hans, who was already getting along in years and who died in 1979 at the age of 62. It was Sweeney who was with him when they put him to sleep by injecting a combination of barbiturates through a vein in his ear. She had grown up to be his keeper.

"I had three years with Hans," she said. "That's all I had. I would have loved to have been with him for his last twenty or thirty years."

Before Sweeney took over as his keeper Hans had been in chains day and night throughout the first half of his long life at the zoo. He was skittish about people, but she got him gentled down enough to trust her. By that time he had severe arthritis from the chains, and the pad of one of his feet was beginning to rot. Finally there was just nothing left to support him, and he collapsed. They hauled his body out of the elephant enclosure with a tow truck, and buried it on the grounds.

Sweeney related all this soberly. Her attention was focused on Thai and Indu now, who were eating a load of roughage, sweeping it up dexterously in their trunks. Thai came over and flopped his trunk over the rail that separated us. I touched it, as he seemed to want, and he coiled it around my arm and nearly yanked me into the pen with him. His bulk, his power, his knowledge were inexpressible. I had that old sentimental boyhood dream: that we understood each other, that my mind converged with his in all the crucial particulars. But I am an adult, and I realized if that fantasy were true I would not have been at the zoo in the first place, staring dumbly at those eyes and at the wide trackless brow between them.

That is perhaps one of the things a human being can finally learn at the zoo. We dominate the animals there, we have their attention, we are in fact their salvation. But we should not expect this to matter to them. On those nights that Dick Bonko talks about, when the monkeys settle down and begin to babble in their wordless speech, they are talking to each other and not to us.

THE PERFECT RIVER

IT IS ONLY A LITTLE RIVER. FROM WHERE THE SAN
Marcos rises abruptly out of the Central Texas rock
to the point at which—as a nineteenth-century poet
phrased it—she gives "her royal hand in marriage to
the waiting Guadalupe" is a distance of only 59 miles.
Well before that union, at an earlier confluence with
the Blanco and an encounter with effluvia from a
wastewater treatment plant, the river begins to lose its
character. Its clear, spring-fed waters are suddenly a
soapy, opaque green; the stream seems bloated, sullied, prodded toward the Gulf.

But within its first few miles, as it meanders through the city limits of San Marcos, the river possesses a simple, radiant beauty. Its waters rise pure and temperate through the porous limestone strata of the vast underground filtration system known as the Edwards Aquifer. Here, at its headwaters, the river has been impounded to form a small body of water known as Spring Lake, but a quarter of a mile downstream it flows again more or less according to its natural inclinations. It runs through the heart of San Marcos — it *is* the heart of San Marcos — and along its way it passes through three public parks, beneath numerous footbridges and trestles, and over a series of broken stone dams, the remains of nineteenth-century mills. Beyond the I-35 bridge the river is deeper, murkier, and perhaps a little wilder, and there are occasional minor rapids.

In its upper stretch the San Marcos is essentially an urban river, relentlessly prettified, its banks shored up by concrete or bordered with philodendrons, its waters stocked with gold-colored carp and Mozambique tilapia, and jammed on summer weekends with rowdy college students slung into inner tubes. But the San Marcos is also a delicate and highly specialized environment for a number of indigenous creatures. Most of them are inconspicuous: a few species of the mothlike caddis flies, which in their larval stage are aquatic; tiny fish like the fountain darter and the San Marcos gambusia; and a salamander, *Eurycea nana*, that occurs in the headwaters of the river and nowhere else in the wide world.

I have seen *Eurycea nana*. A water-quality scientist

named Glenn Longley scooped one up for me from the lake in front of the Aquarena Springs Inn. It was perhaps an inch long, a pale, wriggly form with exotic feather-boa gills. We looked down into the net, where the salamander wriggled in and out of a clump of algae. There did not seem to be much to say about it. "Well," Longley said, shrugging, "that's what they look like."

The creature was returned to the water to browse among the algae for the copepods and other nearly invisible things that it consumes. I had a vague interest in the salamander, but I was stirred by a broader appreciation of the river itself, responding to it not just because it harbored a number of phylogenetic curiosities but because it was simply so pretty. The river is certifiably extraordinary. It has been designated by the government as a "critical habitat" and described in the *Federal Register* as "one of the planet's most precious resources." But I found myself drawn to the river for only the most ordinary reasons: for the way the water sounded and the way it held light. The salamander favored the stream because the water temperature is a fairly constant 72 degrees. The human longing is not so specific, and certainly not so benign in its consequences, but over the millennia it has proved to be no less real. Recent archeological evidence suggests that the river is the oldest continually inhabited site in North America. Despite all the damage we have done to it, our claim to the river is secure.

"A fairyland" was the way one correspondent of the last century described the headwaters of the San Marcos, where a series of first-magnitude springs rises from the Edwards Aquifer. Another imagined it "peopled with laughing water nymphs." The outflow from the springs was more spectacular in those days; the water surged forth from its ancient limestone channels with such force that there was an incessant frothing and fountaining at the surface. Because the lake into which the springs discharge is now deeper, the impounded headwaters of the river are barely riled by the artesian force below.

At its origin, the river runs even with the Balcones Fault, the great geological event that created the distinction between the Texas Hill Country and the plains that slough away to the coast. It was the fault that created the river as well, causing cracks in the limestone through which the rising groundwater worried its way to the open air, enlarging the passages in the process.

The springs have never failed, at least in all the time that humans have kept track of them, and the water has retained its astonishing clarity. If you take one of the glass-bottomed-boat rides at Aquarena Springs, the big tourist sprawl that dominates the headwaters of the river, you can make out—25 feet below the surface—the miniature grottoes along the riverbed through which the high-volume springs discharge.

There are other springs, with less force, that are visible only as ceaseless percolations through the aerated sand covering the limestone. Most of the time the boats skim across a thick bed of aquatic vegetation that is dominated by vertical growths of fanwort and the matted, interwoven strands of *Hydrilla* and riverweed. It's like soaring above the canopy of some surreal rain forest, now and then coming across a clearing. "The white stuff down there is limestone," the guide says, "and the dark stuff is humus—a fancy name for mud." At such points you can see huge undulating caverns in the vegetation, floored with ossified tree limbs and teeming with Rio Grande perch, aquatic turtles, and assorted sunfish to which the guide, assuming her place in the ecology, tosses a dose of food pellets.

The San Marcos is not a "natural" river, unless one is generous enough to consider the meddling attentions that humans have paid it over the years to be a natural process. Although much of the river is choked with plant life, there is no telling how many of the species that inhabit it are indigenous. For years the river was a major source of commercial aquatic vegetation for use in the home aquarium. It was a thriving industry that required a kind of periodic clear-cutting, a harvesting of the cabomba and elodea crops. If, in his travels, a gentleman horticulturist came across a species he thought might look pretty in the river, he'd toss it in and see what happened. Often enough, in the clear, mild water, it would thrive to nightmare proportions.

The river's most prolific introduced species is water hyacinth, a species of floating plant originally from South America. Individually the plants are very picturesque, seemingly just the thing for a burbling, tranquil stream like the San Marcos. They have broad, thick leaves that seem to have been designed to function as airfoils, bulbous stalks filled with pockets of air to keep the plant afloat, and a submerged system of trailing, purplish roots that are reminiscent of soft coral. Each plant produces a prominent flower, but the hyacinths reproduce in a grasslike manner as well, sending out rhizomes and creating new plants, eventually knitting together a floating colony that then becomes part of one of the massive hyacinth blankets that clot the flow of the river whenever it encounters an abutment or a piling.

It was partly to control the water hyacinths that nutrias, the infamous South American water rats, were introduced into the river in the early fifties. Unfortunately, the nutrias left the water hyacinths alone. Otherwise they were like some unstoppable microbe from outer space, ravaging the native vegetation, supplanting indigenous mammals like the woodchuck, and scaring untold numbers of swimmers out of their wits. Over the years the nutrias have proven to be indefatigable pests whose life energies seem to be exclusively devoted to gnawing through the landscape with their big rodent teeth and replicating themselves with astonishing alacrity.

THE RIVER BEGINS ITS PUBLIC COURSE BENEATH an old dam through which the water spills out in an ice-blue, translucent flume. This is an ancestral swimming hole, deep enough in its center to make practicable a rope swing attached to a cypress tree on the bank. There is a restaurant on one bank, student apartments on the other, and a few yards downstream, just above the University Drive bridge, is one of two storm drains that are channeled directly into the river.

I stood there one afternoon at dusk and tried to

imagine what the river had been like two hundred years ago, before the dam had created the falls behind me, before the philodendrons and the water hyacinths and the hordes of bikini-clad teacher trainees from Southwest Texas State University lying indolent and oily in the afternoon sun. The river would have been shallower then (though it is rarely more than eight or ten feet deep now) and lined with the great cypress trees that were eventually cut down and sunk into the riverbed to provide the foundations for the dams that powered the mills along the river a century ago.

But there was no point in trying to imagine it. That particular manifestation of the river is gone, and those of us who have come to love the San Marcos must make do with its present form. And anyway, I was far from being a pure admirer of the river. I wanted it for my own use, just like everyone else, and I was willing to ignore whatever habitual damage I might do to it as I snorkeled along its length, displacing who knew what tiny creatures as my big power fins churned up the silt along its bottom.

I put on my wet-suit top and entered the river near the falls, feeling the first rush of cold and the cyclical thrumming of the agitated water. My notion that day was to swim off in search of the giant freshwater prawn, the elusive crustacean that inhabits the river and was supposedly the basis of a thriving shrimping industry here in the last century. I had seen only one – pickled in a jar in Glenn Longley's office – and had been startled by its size. It was as big as a lobster, with huge meaty claws, and in the preserving fluid its color was a brilliant calcareous white. Since then I had looked for the prawn every time I entered the river, but I had come to the conclusion that it was as myth- ical as the yeti. I let my face mask rest half under the surface, and within the same field of vision I could see a coed on the bank turning over on her stomach and undoing her bikini strap and a stinkpot turtle traveling upstream near the bottom of the river. The stinkpot, aware of my presence, picked up its pace, striding along upon the riverbed in a manner that was at once heavy and buoyant, reminding me of the way astronauts bound, not quite airborne, on the surface of the moon.

The turtle hid among the wide green blades of some water potato plants, and I let the current take me through the shallow, pebbly stretch of the river that led under the bridge and into the concrete sluiceway of Sewell Park, a natural swimming pool where it is customary for Southwest Texas students to relax be- tween classes. Toward the end of this stretch the vegetation was so thick that I had to get out and por- tage myself to a reentry point a hundred yards down- stream near City Park. Here the water was deeper and filled with bass and bluegill and Rio Grande perch. Above the surface there were turtles—cooters—sun- ning themselves on half-submerged limbs. At one point I counted eighteen of them; as I drew closer they all dropped off the log with as little grace as a fall- ing stack of dishes.

A green heron took off from the same log, using its deep, loping wingbeats to propel it to a similar station downstream. There was a yellow-crowned night heron in a tree limb above me, and a rotting snake carcass looped around the piling of a footbridge. The current was stronger here, and like the fish I faced it and watched what it washed downstream. Now and then the fish would lunge at something I couldn't see—a tiny crustacean or water bug—but the only things visible to me were the endless parade of water hyacinths and unidentifiable vegetative debris.

I was washed down to the train trestle at Rio Vista Park, where I wended my way in and out of the pilings, looking under the canopy of water hyacinths for one of the monster prawns. Instead there were crawfish, as lividly red as boiled lobsters, and minute damselfly larvae, structurally indeterminate little beings that looked as if they could as easily evolve into fish as into the flying insects they were destined to become.

I settled to the bottom and as long as my breath lasted watched the lazy, respiring mantle of a half-buried clam, and the bluegill that hovered above their prey and then suddenly dived into the mud like kingfishers. In the mat of water hyacinths above there were sometimes gaps through which the sun penetrated, illuminating the underwater landscape so that it resembled a gloomy storybook illustration of a deep forest glade.

SAN MARCOS IS A CITY OF 23,000 PEOPLE. IT WAS established by fits and starts, first as a short-lived Spanish mission in 1755, later as a Mexican colonial commune that was abandoned in short order because of repeated raids from the local Tonkawas and a flood in 1808. The first Anglo settlers were farmers, veterans of the Texas Revolution and of a later conflict known as the Plum Creek Fight, a decisive horseback battle that effectively chastened the Comanches for a spectacular raid on the coastal town of Linnville. By this time the Tonkawas were in alliance with the settlers against the Comanches, and the ensuing chronicle of San Marcos, to the casual reader interested only in the bloody milestones by which an area develops a "history," seems idyllic and uneventful. One reads about the establishment of businesses, the founding of churches, the building of millraces, and Sunday picnics at the springs.

The economy of San Marcos is still keyed to the stability of the springs that feed the river, but it is a tourist economy now. The city's chief attraction is Aquarena Springs, which, together with a negligible fault-line cavern known as Wonder Cave, siphons off a consistent stream of travelers from I-35. Aquarena Springs began in the twenties, when A. B. Rogers— "a rancher, a sportsman, a leading furniture dealer and undertaker, and a progressive citizen," according to the local newspaper—bought the land surrounding Spring Lake and began to develop the site. He built a hotel and a golf course and over the years outfitted the lake with glass-bottomed boats and an underwater show like the one he had seen at Florida's Weeki Wachee Spring. Rogers' basic philosophy for this enterprise, the park's manager told me, was to "take natural beauty and manicure it."

A variety of exotic things have taken place at Aquarena Springs. Performing seals were brought in, but they did not flourish. Once a four-hundred-pound sea turtle was released in the river, but it promptly sank into the alien biomass and died. On the positive side, Aquarena is proud of the underwater wedding that took place in the submerged theater in 1954, a formal affair in which the groom wore twelve-pound shoes, the bride's skirt was lined with lead hoops, and all "bridal attire" was sprayed with lacquer to "keep its appearance fresh." An event of equal magnitude was the filming of the movie *Piranha*, which featured a now-classic line of dialogue–"Sir, the piranhas are eating the guests!"–spoken on the shores of Spring Lake.

Aquarena now features a sky ride, which angles up from the east bank of the river to the top of the scarp on the other side. There is also a machine called a sky spiral, a rotating observation deck that travels up and down a glaring white metallic shaft that looks like some immense public utility project. Other amenities include the standard "authentic" Western town and a disturbing arcade in which ducks and chickens and rabbits sit in cages and, at the insertion of a coin, proceed in the most dim and perfunctory manner to ring a fire bell or walk a tightrope for their daily niblets. "Welcome to my show," says a sign on these cages. "I am happy and eager to perform for you. My classmates and I were taught at Animal Behavior Enterprises, Hot Springs, Arkansas, using the reward system."

One of the mainstay attractions at Aquarena Springs is Ralph the Swimming Pig, who performs as part of the underwater show. There has been, in fact, a succession of Ralphs; when each one, after about a year, grows too big and persnickety to perform he is–to put it quite bluntly–eaten.

When I attended the underwater show a little Ralph

piglet was being trained off to the side of the Polynesian volcano that is the theater's centerpiece. A college girl in a green sequined bathing suit—an Aquamaid—was trying to entice the creature into the water with a bottle of milk. "Come on," she said, tapping him on the nose with the nipple and then withdrawing it. "Come on, or I'm gonna pop you one."

The performing area for the underwater show is a calm, lucent pool about fifteen feet deep, created by the diversion of a natural spring that rises in the lake behind it. The theater itself is a kind of submarine that, by means of a ballast system that was once the subject of a cover story in *Popular Mechanics*, submerges so that its viewing windows are just below the surface of the water.

On the day I entered the submarine there were few patrons—mostly young parents with bewildered, frenetic toddlers who seemed determined to focus their attention everywhere except on what was happening on the other side of the windows. A young man in a Hawaiian shirt stood at a microphone in the center of the theater and asked us to think of him as our skipper. We observed a feeding frenzy by a group of ducks as we began our descent, and soon we were looking from below at a teeming surface of disembodied paddling feet. Now and then one of the ducks would dive deep for a sinking pellet, fighting hard with those feet to submerge and then finally rocketing to the surface with the buoyancy of a football.

Two "Polynesian witch doctors" named Glurpo and Bubblio jumped into the water from the volcano, pulled two long rubber hoses from its base, and began to breathe from them as they clowned about in the weightless atmosphere of the pool. The South Seas verisimilitude was a little slack. It was apparent when Ralph came onto the scene that the Swimming Pig was not fond of his role. Glurpo coaxed him into the water with a milk bottle and led him around the viewing window. The pig, his wild eyes fixed on the bottle, churned the water with his cloven feet, struggling to keep his snout in the air.

"Glurpo," said the skipper when the pig had completed his rounds, "is going to use his magic on that clamshell and on the mouth of the volcano and bring forth two beautiful, shapely native girls. Hopefully with any luck at all we'll have some beautiful native girls."

A giant clamshell opened and, as in some Botticellian nightmare, an Aquamaid sprang forth. Another soared boldly from the archway in the submerged half of the volcano. Their bathing suits were iridescent; the sequins glittered like fish scales. As they performed acrobatics their blonde hair flowed above their heads like some barely rooted algal mass. The Aquamaids cocked their right legs, arched their backs, and began to rotate, flailing gently with their hands at the water in a manner that suggested the strumming of a harp. Next they demonstrated their prodigious buoyancy control. By inhaling through the hoses, then exhaling, they were able to rise and fall in the pool like counterbalances. Then, retaining just the proper amount of air, they hung motionless, in perfect harmony with the complex hydrodynamics all about them. There was something magnificent about the

Aquamaids. I admired their poise in such an unsettled element, the touching nonchalance with which they sat on giant concrete lily pads and had an underwater picnic, munching on celery and then somehow managing to gurgle an entire twelve-ounce soft drink into their systems.

FOR SEVERAL YEARS AN ARCHEOLOGICAL EXCAVAtion has been taking place in the bottom of Spring Lake, and it is not unusual for patrons of the glass-bottomed boats to look down and see a group of divers picking through a section of river bottom marked off into a grid by red plastic tape.

I spent a few hours here and there working with the archeologists, fanning away the overburden of mud and then picking up flint chips and anything else that seemed to my indiscriminate eye to have significance. The boats came overhead with ceaseless regularity, and whenever I heard the electric whirr of their motors I would look up through fifteen feet of water and marvel at the detail of the faces peering at us through the glass.

At so shallow a depth there is no concern about the bends, and so it's possible for a diver to stay underwater all day, which was the normal operating procedure of the archeologists. It was not unusual for them to put in forty hours a week of total submersion.

Most of them were Southern Methodist University students, supervised by an anthropology professor named Joel Shiner. Shiner was in his sixties, but he looked younger, and he had a glowering, cynical edge that was not unappealing. He first began digging in the lake a few years ago, after a San Marcos acquaintance told him about an abundance of projectile points he had found just below the falls. When Shiner went to look for himself, he found that the reports were correct and that besides the points there were large numbers of exotic rocks—quartz crystals from Arkansas and red metamorphic rocks from West Texas. Since all the artifacts appeared to be in no order whatsoever, it was unclear to Shiner whether they belonged to this site or had merely washed over the falls from their original matrices in the lake.

Shiner got a digging permit from the Texas Antiquities Committee, obtained permission from Aquarena to work in the lake, and gathered up enough in course fees from his archeology students to pay for the gas to and from San Marcos. He had already been conducting make-believe archeology sessions for them in Dallas-area lakes, but now he could put them to work in the field for real—and a gorgeous submerged field at that.

They chose a spot along the ancient river terrace, above the channel where the river must have flowed long before the dam was built and the rising waters diffused its original identity. Shiner wanted to do what he termed a "humanistic" report, to do more than simply catalog the artifacts and their associated strata. He wanted to reconstruct the lives of the Indian cultures that dwelt here, to discover if he could what sort of intangible resources—spiritual resources—they derived from the river.

He had a notion that the exotic rocks he found, rocks that he determined could have arrived at the San

Marcos only by being brought from a great distance and with a certain amount of trouble, had been used as offerings to the springs. "Everybody," he told me, "thinks that Indians are the ideal citizens. They protect the environment and all that crap. So we thought we'd test this hypothesis. Where would the stones be if the Indians were worshiping the springs? Where would the garbage be? If our hypothesis was true, the bottom of the springs would be full of exotic rocks and the bones of virgins, but the garbage would be up on the banks, thrown back from the springs so it wouldn't pollute the water."

In the process of sorting through the evidence in the river bottom, Shiner and his students turned up a treasure trove of artifacts—hundreds of thousands of points and tools dating back through the Paleo-Indian and Archaic periods and suggesting that a sedentary population had lived along the river for 12,000 years. But Shiner concluded that the pretty rocks were not offerings at all but more likely the collection of one or more prehistoric rock hounds. And the garbage that he had expected to find high up on the river terrace wasn't there. It was lower, in the channel. The unseemly truth of the matter was that the Indians had thrown their trash into the springs.

Shiner was not discouraged. In a way, it made these people more real, and it extended the history of human spoilage of the garden spot of the San Marcos River by a good many thousand years. "One way or another," he told me in his Dallas office, which was filled with boxes of projectile points and bison bones and primitive hacking tools, "we're going to make some activity sense out of this site. As people—full-fledged card-carrying people—they had to appreciate the beauty of the place. No way you can avoid it. There's absolutely no reason to believe that these people were inferior in any way. Maybe they didn't make votive offerings to the springs. Maybe the only damn thing the river inspired them to do was sing and dance, but I bet you they sang and danced well. Maybe the springs were not sacred, but that doesn't mean they didn't enjoy looking at them.

"From an economic viewpoint this place was a blessing for the Indians. I'm sure they saw beauty in it. I'd sum it up this way: anybody who left the San Marcos to go someplace else was a damn fool."

THE INDIANS' ROUTINE ABUSE OF THE RIVER WAS part of a natural cycle. While it provides a historical context for our own despoliation, it hardly excuses us. Certainly it is fair to say that most of the solid citizens of San Marcos refrain from tossing their garbage directly into the river, but over the years there has not been a great deal of regard for subtler forms of pollution. During the time I spent in San Marcos, construction around the river was frenetic, while city standards for the control of urban runoff—as well as serious scrutiny of the kinds of projects that should be allowed in the watershed drained by the river—were almost nonexistent.

Things began to change when the residents of an upper-class San Marcos neighborhood known as Springlake Hills noticed red construction flags one day in a streambed near their homes that drains into the headwaters of the river. It is unclear whether the residents' primary motivation in opposing the high-density condominiums scheduled for this site had more to do with environmental matters or with their own property values, but it soon became a cause that stirred the nascent protectionist instincts of a good portion of the citizenry.

The Springlake Hills group, led by a Southwest Texas State University psychology professor named Harvey Ginsburg, widened the arena of concern from their own back yard to the San Marcos River watershed and the entire recharge zone, which is the area in which rainfall and runoff enter the Edwards Aquifer. They asked the city council for a moratorium on all development until the effects of such development could be assessed. For three months Ginsburg bombarded the Planning and Zoning Commission and the city council with data, petitions, and videotapes featuring scenes of the pure, babbling water that was under their stewardship.

In the midst of all this I called on Ginsburg, who lived in a multilevel redwood house that faced the wooded defile that was scheduled to be bulldozed.

"I can take you down many avenues," he said. "Political, environmental, paranormal."

I chose paranormal.

He said there had been a string of what he termed "low-probability coincidences" since the fight had been joined. On the evening of the day he had first tried and failed to get the Planning and Zoning Commission to adopt a moratorium, the creek where all the development was to take place had begun flowing for the first time in three years. At another point Ginsburg and his wife and the two other couples who were most active in the controversy discovered that they all had anniversaries on December 21. And then when the Ginsburgs visited the ruins of Tulum during a trip to Cozumel, a Mexican guide called Pinky told them that the Mayans, who worshiped fresh water, had foolishly constructed a building on top of a cave that housed the spring from which they drew their water. One day the cave roof fell in under the weight of the building. The water was polluted and, Pinky said, "to this day it smells foul."

"Low-probability coincidence," Ginsburg said.

Later that day a colleague of his from the university, a parapsychologist named William Braud, came over to Ginsburg's house and walked with us down to the creek. Braud had brought along a piece of paper on which his wife, who had never seen the creekbed, had jotted down her psychic impressions of it that morning. Ginsburg also had a document, a sort of paranormal deposition that a former student of his had written after Ginsburg took him down to the proposed construction site. The student had suddenly realized he had been to this place before and correctly predicted the location of a group of century plants that grew there.

Ginsburg read the document aloud as we walked down to the creek. "As we meandered into the gully I began to recognize the landscape. . . . We soon came to a place where the earth had fallen away from the higher ground and toward the creek, producing a short, steep ledge."

By the time Ginsburg had read this last sentence he was standing on that short, steep ledge. Below the ledge there was, according to the document, a cave.

I looked at the "cave," which was a depression in the soil that looked as though it had once housed a root system. Meanwhile Braud handed Ginsburg his wife's notes.

"Midden," the paper said. "Indian maiden dressed in white by fish-drying rack. Rock overhang."

"Well, William," said Ginsburg to Braud, "would you say this is a hit?"

"A near-hit, certainly."

I was not quite sure what was going on here. After a while I realized that Ginsburg and Braud felt they were close to proving a hypothesis that this particular place, which was now threatened with high-density condominiums, had once been so powerful or so sacred that it reverberated in the minds of certain "sensitive" souls who had never even seen it. Ginsburg was trying to enter some sort of mystical continuum that ran parallel with the actual course of a river. This was not a concept that would carry much weight with the Planning and Zoning Commission, and whatever psychic sensors I was equipped with had detected no tremors at all. But the idea was appealing; perhaps all that disembodied human energy and longing still hovered at the headwaters of the river, eternally unwilling to leave.

"Let me describe how I feel about this," said Ginsburg when we were back in his house. "I don't know what the coincidences mean. I've just had certain links; I'm not privy to the whole chain. I feel as if I'm a vehicle. I'm just part of the flow. The events are controlling me. I can't explain it.

"I get the feeling that this is a struggle that has occurred before. It's something about building along that river. I get the feeling that at points in time throughout the history of man's living around the river, this struggle has come up many times before. It's a struggle between one group wanting to build something that will damage the environment and another group that believes the environment is sacred."

The controversy raged on through the winter and spring. One day, out of the blue, saying he wanted to spend more time with his family, the mayor quit. A spokesman from the Texas Department of Water Resources got up at a meeting to say the Edwards Aquifer recharge zone was not where everyone thought it was but was located mostly to the west, outside the jurisdiction of San Marcos. On the advice of other professionals, however, the recharge zone was allowed to remain where it was. Finally, a moratorium was adopted, but not before a building permit was issued to the developer who wanted to build the condominiums in the creekbed behind Ginsburg's home. Construction was scheduled to begin in the summer.

EARTH DAY, APRIL 22, WAS A DISMAL, OVERCAST day, and the people who showed up on the banks of City Park to participate in the annual River Cleanup were not legion. There were perhaps twenty or thirty of them.

One of the leaders was Tom Goynes, who owned a canoe livery down the river and was the usual winner of the Texas Water Safari canoe race, which begins at the San Marcos and ends 265 miles later in San Antonio Bay. "I can remember," he said, "about ten years ago it wasn't unusual for schools to let out a half-day for Earth Day. But noooooo, not anymore."

The volunteers took garbage bags and worked up and down the river by canoe or on foot. I put on my snorkeling gear and combed the bottom of the river at City Park. There were hundreds of pop-tops within an area no larger than an average swimming pool, and the bottom was also littered with beer bottle shards, Easter egg shells, Fritos bags, marbles, even a tire tool. It was peaceful, solitary work, and every now and then I would stop and admire the underwater topography, the way a turtle stood motionless underwater on a submerged limb, the constant stream of air bubbles that rose from the whorled stems of the fanwort and from the center of the white flowers that extended sunward on long, fragile stalks.

When I came out of the water I noticed perhaps a thousand young people singing and parading toward City Park, and I was seized for a moment with the inspiring thought that this throng had come to help with the cleanup. But they were only the Derby Day contestants from the college, who had come to the banks of the river for an afternoon of sack races and crab walks.

"Ooooooh," said a girl, a member of an organization named Friends of the River that had helped to organize the cleanup. "If I see any of them throwing down their beer cups . . . *ooooooh*!"

There was a river festival the next Saturday, con-

sisting of an art fair and one or two country bands and
demonstrations of synchronized swimming and children's gymnastics. The highlight of the day was an
aquatic parade through Sewell Park, which comprised
only four or five floats. There was a river queen who
waved to the sparse crowd from a canoe decorated
with crepe paper and pom-poms, an inner tube with
a papier-mâché zebra's head that did not clear the
footbridge and had to be retired, and the Friends of
the River float, which consisted of two canoes tied
together and heaped high with full garbage bags.

ONE NIGHT I WENT ALONG WITH A GROUP OF DIVERS
who, under some official pretext or other, were making a tour of Spring Lake. There was a good moon,
and in the deep holes where the vegetation was kept
cleared, there was already illumination enough for us
to see without lights. I dropped down to the opening
of a high-volume spring and lay basking in the silence
and the half-light and in the steady pressure of the
water that sluiced upward—magically, I thought—from
the depths of the aquifer. How long that water will
continue to flow is an open question. The San Marcos
springs have never failed, but demands on the groundwater that supports them grow every day. San Antonio,
for instance, has no surface-water supply system.
It is cheaper for the city to extract all of its water
directly from the aquifer itself. In another few decades, when the populations of San Antonio and all
the other communities that depend on the aquifer
have dramatically increased, the water table may very
well be too low to feed the San Marcos springs, and

then the river itself will be gone.

We saw a big eel and a spotted gar and several bull-head catfish that were swimming around beneath the submarine theater. I descended to the bottom of the performance pool and remembered the Aquamaids as they had performed their buoyancy skills, hovering there in the water in perfect, ravishing balance. The moonlight played upon the fluted edges of the giant clamshell. Aquarena seemed a mysterious place that night. It seemed almost like a place of worship, the most recent evidence of the ageless, imperfect human infatuation with the river. Our love for such gleaming places has always been ungovernable and devastating.

I stayed in the pool awhile longer, staring through the glass of the submarine into the dark, empty auditorium and then wandering aimlessly around the base of the volcano. Then I swam out of the theater and back into the wellspring of the river. I was looking for the giant freshwater prawn.

GOING INTO
THE DESERT

THERE ARE TWO WAYS TO LOOK AT THE DESERT. You can see it contriving to extinguish life or straining to support it. It all depends upon your mood, and in the desert your mood depends upon water. One of the first symptoms of dehydration is a loss of morale, a disquieting awareness that the landscape has suddenly turned hostile. But to someone who has had plenty of water to drink, whose thoughts are not gloomy, the desert can appear bounteous.

When I was in the Chihuahuan Desert recently, hiking through the volcanic outwash plains or along limestone ridges sodden with midday light, I found myself obsessively scanning the ground for the translucent maroon blooms of the strawberry pitaya. The flowers of this cactus are meant to attract bees and other pollinators, but in that blanched landscape I was hungry for color too. And I knew that on some of these plants the fruit would be ripening. I had more than enough water, and I usually carried oranges as well, so it would have been more considerate of me to pass the fruit by and leave it for the cactus wrens or carpenter ants. But I was not feeling quite so refined. In the desert, the temptation to seek out moisture is irresistible.

I usually found half a dozen blooms on each cactus, though the flowers of the ripe fruits had shriveled to crepe. At that stage the fruits themselves no longer needed protecting, so the dried needles covering the purplish skin could be dusted off with a finger. Peeled, the fruit was a mushy gray ball studded with what looked like poppy seeds – nothing you would think to eat under ordinary circumstances. But the tart pulp tasted, as advertised, like strawberries, or close enough, convincing me that the desert was in some sense benevolent, that for all its austerity it supported pockets of beauty and opportunity. It was an inhospitable place that made me feel welcome.

THE CHIHUAHUAN DESERT IS VAST BUT OBSCURE. Unlike American deserts such as the Sonoran, with its shadeless forests of saguaro cacti, or the Mojave, with its parched playa lakes, the Chihuahuan has no clear emblem to fix it in the popular imagination. (A friend once told me that whenever he hears the words "Chihuahuan Desert" he pictures a pack of hair-less, yipping dogs running through a field of sand dunes.) But like the Sonoran and the Mojave–like the Great Basin, the Sahara, the Namib, the Atacama, the Kalahari–the Chihuahuan is a region of low rainfall and high temperatures, where evaporation exceeds precipitation, where water is the most precious thing imaginable.

There is no real agreement about where the Chihua-huan Desert begins and ends. It is not so much a place as it is a condition. Meteorologists fix its borders according to annual rainfall, biologists according to certain plant or animal associations. Those of us who have no need to be precise about the matter can see the desert's reach clearly enough. It's a great arid swath that extends from the southern borders of the Mexican state of Coahuila all the way up to White Sands National Monument in New Mexico. On some maps it dominates almost all of Texas between El Paso and the Pecos River. On others it is not quite so extensive, but by any reckoning the Chihuahuan covers an immense portion of the Trans-Pecos.

Some ecologists say it consists of 175,000 square miles, making it the largest desert in North America. We may believe them if we like, but the Chihuahuan is so various, so clearly not just one thing, that talk of scale and size can begin to sound irrelevant. In the bajadas and bolsons, in the creosote flats and gypsum dunes, the desert is ferociously real. But you might find yourself in a high mountain oasis filled with ever-greens and clouds, or beside a deep, clear pool fringed with luxuriant grass, and wonder just what the desert has to do with these places at all. It is correct, say the ecologists, to think of the badlands and the lush islands as all of a piece, as part of the same biome, the same xeric province. When described in such eco-speak terms, the desert can seem ambiguous. But when you travel to the low, hot, waterless places, its hold is unmistakable.

In the extreme lowlands, hardly anything grows higher than your waist, and when the sun is high its light falls hard and straight. Beneath this burdensome light the desert floor has the feel of a sea bottom—a place ruled by a crushing atmosphere, where life is stunted and scarce. It is not an easy place to love at that time of day, when everything visible seems washed out or fixed in some monotonous middle distance.

"Here in the desert you have to train yourself to look for detail," Alan Brenner, the education director at the Chihuahuan Desert Research Institute in Alpine, told me one day as we walked along in such a landscape. "The big picture is spectacular, and the little picture is spectacular, but the picture in between is daunting to most sensibilities."

The flat plain was paved with volcanic cobbles, and the in-between picture that Brenner spoke of consisted almost entirely of creosote bush, the world champion desert scrub. These spindly, tensile plants, with their tight little leaves, fanned out in every direction, as evenly spaced as the trees in a fruit orchard. There was something hypnotic in their regularity. Like clouds that arrange themselves in sky-spanning columns, the creosote seemed to hint that nature was filled with infinite patterns that the human eye could not quite detect.

Creosote is an invader. It makes its way into environments where other plants have given up hope, sends out its shallow roots, and thrives. Creosote began its conquest some time after the last ice age, when what is now the Chihuahuan Desert was a woodland filled with piñon, juniper, and oak. As the ice sheets retreated and the climate began to dry out, the forests tended to give way to desert grasslands and finally to desert scrub. How desolate any particular region became depended largely on its elevation, with the high mountain environments surviving as relics of a greener time.

In the lower evelations, where piñon and juniper feared to tread, the field was left to things like creosote and cacti that had a decided preference for godforsaken ground. A cactus deals with its arid surroundings by soaking up water in times of plenty and storing it within. Because a cactus must protect that store of water from evaporation, it is cautious about opening its stomata, the minute pores on its surface through which it gathers oxygen.

Creosote, on the other hand, is so efficient at slurping up every molecule of moisture in the vicinity that it has no need to store water. Furthermore, its small, waxy leaves help prevent evaporation, making it feasible for the plant to be on-line during the hottest part of the day. When a drought comes and not even the wily creosote can find water, it drops its leaves and hunkers down. One theory about why the plants are so evenly spaced holds that the dead leaves contain a chemical that may suppress other plants that might be trying to gain a foothold beneath them. Another opinion is that a creosote bush extracts so much water from the soil that nothing else can survive within its immediate radius.

AS I WALKED THROUGH THE CREOSOTE THAT afternoon, the temperature rose above one hundred. I was used to humidity, so the dry heat was disconcerting. I had no sensation of thirst, and because the sweat evaporated almost immediately from my skin I was barely aware that I was perspiring. But while walking in that environment I was losing about a quart of water an hour, and whenever I went too long without topping off my body moisture I could feel my mental acuity begin to deteriorate.

Things can go wrong quickly in the desert if the water the body loses through evaporation isn't replaced. A friend of mine, when he was seventeen, came close to dying of dehydration when he got lost near the Chinati Mountains. Only a few hours after drinking the last of his water, he remembers, he began to feel dizzy and depressed. By late that afternoon he was having hallucinations. "They were very, very vivid," he recalled. "In the first one my dad appeared on horseback and asked me if I was exhausted. He was dressed exactly the same as when I'd last seen him. I could hear his horse. It was so incredibly real that when he disappeared I was madder than ever."

By evening he had begun to lose his motor control and could not even manage to bring his hands up to break his frequent falls. He fell asleep twice but each time began immediately to dream about water. In the dreams he would raise the water to his mouth, but just as he was taking a drink he would swallow in his sleep. The pain in his throat was so bad it woke him.

He tried to drink his urine but could not make himself do it. His swollen tongue hurt as if he'd bitten it. All he could think about was what it would be like to take a drink. When he was found the next afternoon and the great moment finally arrived, his throat was so swollen he could not swallow—the water just trickled down so that he could barely feel its presence. It was hours before he was even able to experience the sensation of relief. For two days he lay in a room drinking pitchers of iced tea.

Humans can adapt to desert life only by caution, by careful attention. Our surest survival strategy is an instinct to stay out of the sun. This is a trait we share with many other desert creatures, no matter how specialized their own evolutionary tactics have become. The kangaroo rat, for instance, spends its days beneath the earth in a deep burrow, whose opening it carefully plugs with dirt to keep out the searing heat. It sleeps with its tiny paws in front of its snout in order to trap the refuge's precious humidity and hold it close. The creature comes out at night, a nervous, bounding thing with a twitching nose. Its head in proportion to the rest of its body is immense, equipped with voluminous cheek pouches that are meant to be filled with seeds. The legs appear spindly but are strong enough to launch the kangaroo rat in sometimes spectacular leaps across the starlit desert floor. The tail is long and thick, often tufted at the end; it is used for balance and to keep the rat stable in midair as it smites rivals with its feet.

In its evolutionary repertoire, the kangaroo rat has one extraordinary trick: it does not consume water. There are other desert inhabitants—rabbits and so forth—that rarely drink "free" water but get their moisture allotments from fruits and succulent plants. But the kangaroo rat is a far step ahead. Deep in its industrious little body, mixing the starches from seeds it consumes with the oxygen in the air, it manufactures its own water. All animals do this to some degree but at nowhere near a level that would be sufficient for survival. The kangaroo rat, however, is phenomenally thrifty with the water it produces. It hardly sweats, and its urine is five times as concentrated as that of humans. Under extreme deprivation in heartless laboratory experiments, a few kangaroo rats have been induced to drink water, but in the normal course of their lives they never need to consider such a drastic measure.

As I walked across the desert I thought of the kangaroo rat, a little organic still that was bundled up in the darkness below my boots. There were other burrows, filled with other slumbering forms that were waiting for the earth to become habitable again. The wolf spider's burrow was small and guarded by a silky rampart that the spider had spun around its circumference. I peered into the larger burrows, trying to imagine what sort of creature was down in the cool and nearly absolute dark: a badger, a cottontail, a rattlesnake; maybe a carnivorous grasshopper mouse, which is in its own way as predaceous and far ranging as a mountain lion, controlling a hunting range of eight acres. There were toads down there and dessicated fairy shrimp waiting for months or even years to be reconstituted by the touch of water.

Lizards darted across my path as I walked through the scrub. Lizards are generally more heat-tolerant than snakes, though like all reptiles they have no means of regulating their temperature internally. When it gets too hot or cold, they remove themselves to a more bearable place. For now, the desert floor was fine. One sort—the greater earless—ran in short bursts, pulling up every few feet with their backs stiffened and their black-and-white-striped tails curved upward like the stinger of a scorpion. They held this pose patiently, as if they wanted to be admired.

The more colorful whiptail lizards were swifter, their movements as elusive to the eye as shooting stars. Chihuahuan lizards tend to be small game compared with some that live in the Sonoran. There you have stocky chuckwallas and desert iguanas. The venomous Gila monster never enters the Texas desert, though many Texans still tread fearfully, expecting it to rush out of the brush at any moment and lock its jaws around their flesh. (Although Gila monsters are not within our purview, I can't refrain from passing on these first-aid instructions printed in Peggy Larson's valuable guidebook, *The Deserts of the Southwest:* "Remove the lizard from the bite as rapidly as possible, as the lizard continues to chew venom into the victim while it remains attached. It may be difficult to disengage the reptile. . . . Its jaws may be pried open with pliers, etc. A strong tasting or smelling liquid [such as alcohol, chloroform, gasoline] may be poured into its mouth, or a flame may be applied to the lizard's jaw. [Refrain from using the gasoline and the flame methods in conjunction!]")

Fortunately, a visitor to the Chihuahuan Desert requires neither pliers nor chloroform. At least some lizards here—a few species of the little whiptails—make up in weirdness for what they may lack in size or notoriety. Members of these species are all females, and they have developed the knack of reproducing themselves without the participation of males.

Such dynasties begin with a materfamilias, possibly the female progeny of a chance mating of lizards from two similar but distinct whiptail species. Like a mule, which is the product of the union of a horse and a donkey, this lizard is a hybrid. But a mule is sterile, whereas a female whiptail can make carbon copies of herself. Nobody's quite sure how she does it. Apparently she produces a chemical that aggravates the membranes of her eggs and makes them cleave, a job that in a more traditional fashion would be accomplished by the sperm of a male lizard. The egg develops, but without the sperm it has no new genetic input, and so out pops a duplicate of the mother.

Sometimes the desert feels as if it is governed by such alien mores, by unfathomable principles and practices, by secrets. But the desert is a human environment too, the frontier of privation to which we are always peculiarly receptive. We speak of "going into the desert," and we mean nothing less than seeking our true selves. It is a place where one goes to be scoured and purified, to await visions.

One day I hiked across the flats to an isolated promontory of intrusive rock. On a ledge twenty or thirty feet above the ground were petroglyphs, and nearby were narrow grooves that the Indians had cut into the rock and used to sharpen their arrow points and straighten the shafts. The ground was littered with flint chips, and there were deep metates in the rock, some filled with dirty rainwater, that were as smooth and precise as if they had been drilled by a machine. Through my binoculars I looked across the drab flats to the foothills of a desert mountain range and saw, at that slightly higher elevation, the withered bloom stalks of agaves and scattered tufts of death-defying grass. It was a classic Chihuahuan Desert vista, and I thought of how the rock on which I was standing must have been a landmark and a refuge in this region for thousands of years.

The earliest desert peoples here were hunter-gatherers—or, as one author insists, gatherer-hunters, since most of their diet consisted of food that had been found rather than killed. We know this through the study of coprolites, which were discreetly described to me as "fossilized doo-doo." Coprolite samples taken from a rock shelter that was inhabited during the Archaic Period—from about 9000 B.C. to A.D. 1000—indicate that the people who lived there were inspired omnivores. "The eclectic diet was a complete surprise," writes Glenna Dean, one of the archeologists involved in the survey. "We can imagine a daily rodent eaten along with prickly pear pads and one or another type of fruit or crunchy as a side dish—a blue plate 'rat sandwich.' "

Some parts of the desert were more hospitable than others. Near Presidio, at the fertile junction of the Rio Conchos and the Rio Grande, there lived a farming people called the Jumanos, who represented the advancing edge of the Puebloan civilizations of New Mexico and Colorado. But that sort of pastoral existence was beyond the reach of most desert Indians, who foraged on the land and hunted in the high mountains for game.

"The multitude is innumerable in every direction," stated a report to the king of Spain in 1679 concerning the Indian population of the Chihuahuan Desert. The names of these peoples—Tepeguanes, Conchos, Saliñeros, Cabezas, Tobosas, Coahuileños, Chisos—have slipped from history, but their presence was very real. They lived within the boundaries of Spanish ambition, and they fought hard against the constant press of would-be conquistadores. In the end, many of them were exterminated or sold as slaves to the mine operators of Nueva Vizcaya, but their desert homeland remained, in essence, unconquered. The Spanish could barely tolerate this wilderness, much less hold it as a secure part of the empire. It was the Apaches and later the Comanches who were the true rulers, though finally their reign was vivid but short-lived.

Wagon trails were opened across the desert, linking —sometimes more in theory than in practice—the cities of Chihuahua and El Paso with Gulf ports like Indianola and New Orleans. A railroad appeared. There were a few modest silver strikes, along with quicksilver mines and real estate speculation and factories for rendering wax from the candelilla plant. But none of that could put an end to the desert's isolation or alter its character.

Ranching, however, went a long way toward changing the face of the desert—by creating more of it. The process started during the First World War, when many ranchers, tempted by an improved market for beef, overburdened their land with livestock. The complex desert grasslands turned to simple desert scrub. J. O. Langford, an early homesteader, wrote poignantly of this change. A malaria victim, he had moved with his young family to the Big Bend area in 1909 to recover his health and found a kind of peace in the desert that he was fated never to know again. The border turmoils of 1913 forced him to retreat to El Paso, where he operated a filling station and where his little daughter, who had survived rattlesnakes and bandits in the desert, was electrocuted while playing on a swing. Years later he managed to move his family back to the desert, but it was not the same. "Where once I'd thought there was more grass than could ever be eaten off," he wrote, "I found no grass at all. Just the bare, rain-eroded ground. . . . Somehow, the brightness seemed gone from the land."

TOWARD MIDAFTERNOON I FOUND MYSELF ON TOP of a miniature mesa whose summit looked as if it had been hammered flat by the force of the sun. All around me grew lechuguilla, the fiercest plant in the desert. Its Spanish name translates to "little lettuce," but what it resembles more is an armor-plated artichoke. The lechuguilla's leaves are strong and sharp, and on the slopes that the plant favors, its leaves point uphill in palsied, clawlike clusters. To a person picking his way down such a slope, the plants can appear bloodthirsty and grasping. Lechuguilla lives at least three or four years, husbanding water in its thick leaves, before finally erupting in a bloom stalk that can be ten feet high.

I was too late for the lechuguilla's yellow flowers, but the desert slopes were filled with dried-out stalks that either had fallen to the ground or were on the verge of collapse. I picked up a few and used them as poles to set up a tarp. There was no shade for miles, nothing besides the thin lechuguilla stalks capable of casting a shadow, and I didn't realize until I slipped under the tarp how deeply I wanted to be out of the sun. I was overcome by a comfort that in any other climate I would have considered marginal.

I lay there all afternoon, torpid and unthinking. Nothing moved along the ground except for a desert millipede, a chain of compressed coils and feathery legs bound together by some animate need. The shadow of a turkey vulture passed over my foot, and I looked up to see the bird not far overhead, suspended in the air with no more consideration than it took for me to lie on the earth.

Turkey vultures are not really desert birds. They're equally at home in the tropics, where their acute sense of smell—rare for vultures—helps them locate carrion beneath dense forest canopies. But you cannot imagine the desert without their forms cruising overhead, soberly patrolling for signs of death.

Young turkey vultures are said to make good pets. They like to be handled and follow their owners around like dogs. And there is something about the look of a fledgling buzzard that exerts a strange pull on the human heart. Its downy, ungainly body contrasts disturbingly with its naked head, which makes it seem as cold-blooded as a pirate. A vulture, of course, is no more malevolent than any other creature, but not many people can afford it anything but grudging tolerance. We don't like the way it makes its living in general, and there's always the faint worry that one day it may be practicing its trade over our remains.

For such a task it is splendidly endowed. Its wings are useless for aerial pursuit, but perfect for hovering in the thermals, from which the vulture scans the panoramic stillness below. A turkey vulture's feet are equipped with claws, but they're not strong enough to grab a bird in flight. They're for holding on to a carcass while the vulture probes inside, ripping and chomping with its heavy-duty bill. It should come as no surprise that the vulture has a powerful digestive system. Chicks grow up eating regurgitated carrion provided by their parents and are able to process seemingly implacable items like bone and hide in a few days. Even with that iron stomach, though, the turkey vulture occasionally gets queasy. When stressed or frightened, it throws up. This happens frequently on highways, where birds working a road kill tend not to notice an oncoming car and have to scramble frantically to get airborne. The prudent thing for a driver to do in this situation is slow down, since vulture vomit is one of the foulest substances on earth. I'm told that if a vulture upchucks on your windshield you might as well sell the car.

At the other end of the avian spectrum are the minute lucifer hummingbirds that venture into the desert to feed on the nectar of flowering plants. During my long siesta I kept my eyes on a blooming century plant—rare for this low elevation—that stood in dramatic isolation fifty yards away. I was waiting for a hummingbird to stop by, but none ever did, and the more I waited, the more unlikely it seemed that such a fragile little bird could fly across this austere landscape without being fried in midair by the sun.

Unlike vultures, which loll about on desert updrafts and hardly move their wings except to alter their course, hummingbirds are an unceasing eruption of energy. It makes your pulse race just to watch them. Their own wings churn the air like rotors, and while the wings whizz frantically about its body the little bird is stabilized, able to hover in front of a flower and draw nectar into its long, grooved tongue, which, when not in use, lies coiled in the hummingbird's cranium like a fire hose.

The aerodynamic maneuvering is costly, and a hummingbird spends a good deal of time refueling. Though they supplement their diet with protein, using a forcepslike bill to pluck spiders from webs, hummingbirds subsist primarily on nectar. In the case of the century plant, they feed mainly on leftovers, since this particular agave has established an agreeable relationship with the Mexican long-nosed bat. The bats have even more prodigious tongues than hummingbirds do, made of erectile tissue that can become swiftly tumescent. A biologist, Donna Howell, has filmed bats feeding on agave flowers, and the slow-motion footage reveals a great amount of indecorous slurping. The bats are favored customers of the century plant, because during nocturnal feeding flurries they scatter pollen to other flowers or collect it on their fur. Howell found that the bats always leave a certain amount of nectar behind; they receive a message through some inscrutable channel that the energy expended in draining the flowers is greater than the fuel intake. The amount of nectar left in the flower is negligible for the bats, but it's well worth a stop the next day for the hummingbirds, who are used to tanking up microliter by microliter. The precise hummingbirds are no help in pollination, but the century plant, perhaps in some fashion exhausted after its nighttime rendezvous with the bats, does not seem to begrudge them.

IT IS ONLY WHEN THE SUN IS LOW ON THE HORIZON that the desert takes on texture, becomes alluring in a conventional way. The shallow, sun-washed drainages begin to appear deep and inviting, places of refuge. The bleached arroyos that in the full light of day are nothing but impediments, that seem to crisscross the desert floor without logic, suddenly are charged with significance and possibility. Subtle contours in the land become apparent, and in the variable light the solid components of the desert seem to shift and change shape like clouds. The wind is up. The temperature is down. The body, whose resources have been preoccupied all afternoon with preventing heatstroke, begins to make adjustments. As evening deepens, you can feel the blood enlivening your brain once again, and you feel that, instead of coming to the end of a tiring day, you are rising from a long and stupefying sleep.

A little nighthawk, a poorwill, flies low over the scrub, emitting plaintive bursts of song. There is a watery, musky smell—the diluted essence of skunk—that indicates a javelina is nearby, blundering about with its inferior eyesight. The subdued colors of the desert fade, except for a strawberry pitaya flower, which continues to burn like a flame until there is no light to support it. Mosquitoes, bred in the drying puddles of a nearby arroyo, circle ceaselessly around your head and bore into your eardrums with their whine. It is the last thing you want in this contemplative landscape, to be annoyed. Tonight the desert is as petty as it is powerful—filled with minuscule, bothersome life as well as silent beasts who keep their thoughts to themselves as they stalk their prey on the ground or from the air. Vega is bright, and Venus rises with the Twins beneath the moon. Half of the moon is in shadow, and half is startlingly clear, glowing with eerie intensity, like the all-seeing eye of an owl. That is the real desert. In comparison with the moon, even the volcanic soil beneath your sleeping bag feels alive and impatient. A large beetle scuttles across your hand, mistaking it for a rock, for one more silent manifestation of the terrain.

THE DESERT RAINY SEASON, SUCH AS IT IS, OCCURS in the summer. The higher elevations can receive as much as twenty inches of rainfall a year, but in the lowlands the total is much less. The Chihuahuan Desert, by and large, lies beyond the reach of serious precipitation. Tucked away in the heart of a huge landmass, the desert is not on the itinerary of the big seasonal storms spawned in the Gulf and the Pacific. The rain systems that come its way are likely to be trapped by the mountain ranges that border the Chihuahuan for almost its whole extent. There the storms are broken up, the moisture-laden air retreating to windward and the rain shadow below receiving only a hot, evaporative wind.

But in the summer, thunderstorms often find their way to the desert. They're brief and volatile, drenching the unprepared soil and filling the dry washes with fast-moving sheets of floodwater. All sorts of things crawl out of the ground then, ready to feed and mate, to get on with a life that may have been held in suspension for months. I drove along a desert road recently after a rain. From my open window I could hear the bleating of what were probably spadefoot toads, and millipedes by the hundreds were crossing the road. Perhaps it was my imagination, but they all seemed to be crossing at the same angle; it was as if they were all single expressions of some larger impulse, some thought.

A desert tarantula was crossing the road as well. I stopped the car and watched it. It was about six inches long and moved slowly, probing with a pair of forelegs. Each step it took seemed reasoned. I put my hand in its path, and it crawled up to my wrist before thinking better of it and moving back to the asphalt. Tarantulas are capable of inflicting a painful, mildly venomous bite, but if they are handled with consideration they're extremely forbearing. Their abdomens are covered with a mat of short, fine hairs—irritating to certain predators—which they can shed when provoked.

Odds were that this tarantula, being on the prowl, was a male. If he was sexually mature, he was at least ten years old. His future was cloudy, however, given female tarantulas' propensity for eating their mates.

Tarantulas live on insects and other spiders, but they're fully capable of pouncing on a creature as large as a mouse and knocking it out with their venom. After that, they pump it full of digestive juices and leisurely suck away its insides. The tarantula's mortal enemy is the tarantula hawk, a wasp that stings the spider until it is comatose, then drags it off and uses it as a nest. When the wasp's larvae hatch, they begin to consume the still-living spider, bringing a protracted end to a life that may have spanned 25 years.

As I drove I saw roadrunners, hunched forward in a kind of Groucho Marx posture, speed across the highway in front of my car, sometimes taking a short hop to the summit of a scrubby mesquite. A large snake, bright pink, hurled itself at my tires. I jerked the steering wheel back and forth and careened all over the road trying to avoid it, feeling a little put out at the effort. I could have run over the snake and no jury in the world would have convicted me, but when I looked into the rearview mirror and saw it escaping into the brush unharmed I had to congratulate myself on my evasive driving skills. But the larger satisfaction was in not having caused a meaningless death, in not having insinuated my Buick Regal into the desert's balance of peril.

Up ahead a jackrabbit was perched tensely on the

side of the road, waiting for whatever signal it needed to break and run. Its ears were enormous—they looked as if they were intended to gather data from outer space. The animal itself appeared gaunt and tested. When it finally took off, it crossed the road with astonishing speed, bounding forward on its immense hind legs. When it reached the other side it ran in zig-zags through the creosote and vanished under my gaze.

A jackrabbit is not a rabbit. It's a hare. Unlike rabbits, which are born naked in burrows, hares come into the world covered with fur, their eyes open, their minds already factoring the chances of escape over open ground. Jackrabbits survive by vigilance and speed. They live alone, sleeping in little scraped-out depressions in the earth called forms. They're vegetarians, and the tiny identations you often find along the edges of prickly pear pads are evidence that a jackrabbit has been feeding there.

Further on, another shape crossed the road. This was a canine, and I almost gasped at the thought it might be a wolf. Its haunches were scrawny, but it was larger than any coyote I'd ever seen, and it had a thick, reddish ruff at its neck. Its wildness was breathtaking. As it scrambled over a rise it reminded me of one of those wolves in Disney cartoons who appear on a mountaintop, ragged and lordly, in a flash of lightning.

But it could not have been a wolf. The last wolves in the Chihuahuan Desert disappeared, as far as anyone can tell, sometime in the early seventies, shot or crowded out or poisoned by sodium fluoroacetate. What I saw doubtless was a big coyote, but I didn't want to make myself believe it. I stopped the car and got out, savoring the image, and saw something even more arresting.

At first it seemed to be a rainbow, hovering low in a desert hollow three hundred yards away. It had rained a short time earlier, and the air was charged and complex, so a rainbow would not have been out of place. But that was not what this was. I could make out a few subtle gradations of the spectrum, but the phenomenon itself was a wonderful green light that had none of the phantom qualities of a rainbow. It was so well defined that I felt I could walk up to it and size it with a tape measure. I watched it, expecting something more. It was exactly the sort of supernatural light I had imagined as a boy in Catholic school, a backdrop from which the Virgin Mary might appear and say, as she always did in her apparitions, "Do not be afraid, my child."

The intricate atmospheric conditions that were causing this light could not be sustained for long, and in a moment it simply vanished, like water evaporating on a hot rock. I stared at the little arc of sky where it had been, greedy for something more, for some further revelation. I found it hard to take such a numinous display in passing. There was nothing mystical about it—it was neither hallucination nor vision—but when it was gone it lingered happily in my imagination, and I felt myself woven a little deeper into the fabric of the desert.

AFTER SEVERAL DAYS OF HIKING AROUND IN THE desert I began to wonder what it would be like to walk again in a landscape where every footstep did not have to be a considered proposition. One afternoon, on a rugged talus slope near the entrance to a narrow canyon, I came to the conclusion that it was not worth the effort to walk anymore. I felt like a contortionist as I tried to dodge the profusion of thorny plants surrounding me. Lechuguilla, prickly pear, pencil cactus, bloodroot, catclaw acacia, ocotillo—they were all savagely defending their precious stores of moisture, and I was sick of it. At that moment the desert was unsettling and grim, a place that preferred death over life. The bristly plants clung defiantly to the desert's surface, but if the desert itself had any one desire, it was to become a void.

To a degree, that is the course of things. The Chihuahuan Desert is threatened with "desertification." The more it is abused and degraded, the more it becomes a desert. To understand the tragic nature of this process, it's important to remember how intricate an environment a desert is. Deserts are second only to rain forests in their ability to support a wide variety of species. They have a range of climate and topography that creates more ecological niches than could exist in a temperate zone. But this natural diversity is fragile, and when it is stripped away, the desert loses all character and relief and becomes a monotonous, barren land.

The threat comes from every direction. The grasslands are overgrazed, and in their place rise creosote and mesquite. Cowbirds that follow cattle onto the ranges lay their eggs in vireo nests, where the raucous cowbird chicks persuade the vireo mothers to feed them instead of their own young. A real estate development destroys bat habitat, and because there are fewer bats to pollinate the century plant, its population declines. Running water is channeled or used up. Imported vegetation like salt cedar dries up a spring with its powerful hydraulics. The steady economic pressure on ranchers forces them to sell their land, which is subdivided for development. More wells are drilled, more water is depleted. More pesticides and contaminants are cycled into the food chain.

The Chihuahuan Desert Research Institute, which is headquartered in a portion of the science building at Sul Ross State University in Alpine, has been gamely trying to educate people through the years about the desert's variety and fragility. It's not an easy job, because the desert has no real constituency. People look out their car windows at the endless creosote plains and see emptiness. What they are looking at, however, is not the real desert in its vital and complicated glory. What they are looking at is what the desert has become.

THERE ON THE TALUS SLOPE, HEMMED IN BY SPINES and needles, I was feeling less appreciative of the desert than I might have been. Maybe my cautious steps were a little exaggerated, but I was in one of those moods. The desert did not seem hostile, simply unconcerned about my welfare, and that was enough to make me feel vulnerable and alone.

So far, it had been a wet summer for this part of the desert, and the ocotillo plants I encountered – tall shrubs made up of dozens of thorny stems – were filled with leaves. A north wind began to whip the stems into motion, and I looked up to see the sky filled with separate thunderstorms, moving as ponderously as supertankers in a crowded harbor. All at once the atmosphere began to deepen, and the scraggly, denuded mountains in the distance turned steel-blue. I moved down to the flats, thinking to get back to the car, which was four miles away across the pathless scrub. I expected at any moment to be caught in a downpour, but soon it became apparent that it wasn't going to rain, that the great thunderheads were merely going to shuffle about on the horizon and disappear.

So I sat down to watch the spectacle of rain flirting with the desert. I took my Walkman out of my backpack, listened to Elvis Costello's *Imperial Bedroom* for a while, then switched to Schubert. The music brought the desert up a notch, or so I imagined. It imposed feeling and reason on a landscape that otherwise could be frighteningly neutral. Protected by Schubert, I perceived the desert's scale and stirrings in human terms. It seemed to want music as much as it wanted rain, and I felt that if I turned up the volume, life would explode from every burrow, from every pore in the calcified soil.

But after a point—when the ants near my feet appeared to be marching with renewed purpose and the wiry creosote stems were swaying in rhythm—the orchestration got to be too much. I took off the earphones and shrank right back into place—just one more creature with an overworked evaporative system, with no greater understanding of the desert than what my senses were able to tell me. Two Scott's orioles were singing to each other across the flats.

When I stood up I startled a grasshopper on a nearby mesquite, who took flight with a whirring sound that resembled the rattle of a snake. It reminded me to be cautious walking back. The thunderstorms were far away now, and the excitement had gone out of the atmosphere. There was only the sun, holding forth as usual. I took a long drink of warm water and felt just fine.

ISLA DEL PADRE

AN OLD MAN WHO WAS HANGING OUT AT A BAIT stand in Flour Bluff asked me if I was driving to Padre Island and if I would give him a ride across the causeway. His face was badly sunburned, and he wore an old corduroy sport coat and a cap with gold braid on the bill.

"They call me Half-Acre," he said as we started across the laguna. "I worked for Army intelligence during the war. Still do, in fact." He looked out the window as a great blue heron that was standing at the water's edge spread its wings, executed a deep curtsy, and shoved itself aloft. Behind the bird a board sailor was hotdogging in the shallows, riding with his feet on the rim of the board and pointing the sail ahead of him, clew first, like a weapon.

I wanted to ask Half-Acre if he had ever gone across on the old causeway, whose wooden pilings were still visible in the shallow water, but he was busy talking about Russian submarines, coded messages, and something about a Walther handgun that he had stolen from Hitler. Up ahead was the Intracoastal Canal, and soaring above it was the elegant span that replaced the swing bridges I had known as a kid. At the top of the new bridge I let my eyes drift from the road and looked out over the Laguna Madre – the Mother Lagoon. Its surface was marked by oyster reefs and spoil islands, and to the south the mild, milky-blue water bled into the horizon. Ahead, where the road touched down again, was Padre Island.

"I'm a doctor too," Half-Acre was saying. "Psychiatrist. I've worked with the finest psychiatrists in the world. They'd send me their toughest patients, the ones they couldn't help. I was able to cure them all but one, and I married her. She got her head blown off, though."

I was trying to decide whether to inquire further when we reached Half-Acre's destination, another bait stand, on the narrow shell bank between the causeway and the water. He thanked me for the ride and walked inside, leaving me to wonder if anywhere in the world there was a better environment for such a grizzled old salt than Padre Island.

"A wretched, barren sandbank," wrote a doctor who

was shipwrecked here in 1846, "destitute of animals, and nothing found existence here, but disgusting sand crabs, and venomous insects."

No longer wretched, no longer barren, no longer destitute, the island is still, in its mysterious essentials, much the same place that castaway described. It is the world's longest barrier island, running for 115 miles along the Texas coast and guarding the fertile waters of the laguna from the open Gulf. At its north end, near Corpus Christi, it is sporadically developed. There is a county park, a few beachfront condos and hotels, a back-island residential community with canals and an open-air church – all of it giving way soon enough to Padre Island National Seashore, which is a wild stretch of 67.5 miles acting as a psychic counterbalance to the booming resort city of South Padre Island at the southern end.

Even so, "island" seems too grand a term for the place. It is, in fact, a sandbank, half desert and half mosquito-ridden grass flats, a wayward spit of land that, depending on your circumstances, could be either a purgatory or a paradise.

My circumstances that April day were pretty good. I was oufitted. Since I was going to journey down the length of the island, over dicey shell beaches and stretches of soft sand that could ingest a car up to its headlights, I had rented a four-wheel-drive Blazer. I had a Sears tent designed by Sir Edmund Hillary, a few cans of Sweet Sue Chicken 'n Dumplings, four bottles of Gatorade on ice, and a fishing license that I had sworn out at a local 7-Eleven.

Here, near the tip of the island, the tidal flats were

overgrown with condominiums, and the island road was lined with sales offices, convenience stores, and windswept shell boutiques. I headed off north, to Access Road 3, an old haunt. The access road led to the beach just below Corpus Christi Pass. At one time, the pass was a natural channel, as much as thirty feet deep in some places, that cut across the width of the island and separated Padre from Mustang Island, which runs north from this point 23 miles to Port Aransas. The pass is only a remnant now, a wide break in the dunes that has filled in over the years with hard-packed sand and a few stray tidal pools, but its topographical importance still holds. This is where Padre Island officially begins.

Today was a Sunday, but the sky was overcast and there was a lingering trace of winter in the air that had kept most of the weekend beachgoers home. The few cars on the beach were widely spaced, parked broadside to the surf. Despite the overcast, people were doggedly sunbathing, stretched out on their hoods with their faces turned to the Gulf.

In the old days, that was about as crowded as Padre Island ever seemed to get. I remember being aware as a child of its vast desolation. It was a place that compelled attention but withheld comfort. The relentless wind, the noise of the surf, the salt sting of the water in my eyes—all those things seemed vaguely hostile. I had not been to any other seacoasts, but I imagined them as tamer, less isolated, less demanding. With more effort than ever seemed worthwhile, my mother would set up a folding metal table and tablecloth on the lee side of the car, and during the long afternoon

we would fish or bodysurf or sit in the car eating potato chips, glad to have a place of refuge. I felt hounded
by the wildness of Padre Island, but in the evenings
I began to be seduced by it. We would sit in folding
chairs as the moon came up, not bothering to move
as the evening tide sluiced below us, the chairs sinking
and shifting into the unstable sand. The insufferable
wind by then had modulated to a cool sea breeze, and
the waves were more regular and subdued. The track
of the moon on the water was so bright and solid it
looked like it could support your weight. The adults,
sipping their drinks, would be moved to platitudes
about beauty and infinity. The children were naturally
suspicious of such sentiments, but like our elders
we were both lulled and aroused by the spectacle
before us. I would stare out beyond the whitecaps,
expecting at any moment to see something really
good: a breaching whale, or the suddenly exposed hull
of a sunken caravel. Looking out to sea across that
blinding streak of moonlight, I thought of Padre Island
as a rare place, a place where some cosmic payoff was
always near at hand.

Since those days the island has, as its promoters say,
"come a long way," but its identity remains rooted
in age-old solitude. Behind the imposing beachfront
developments at the north end, along the tidal shore
of the laguna, you can still find the sites of Karankawa
camps—grass flats littered with arrow points and shell
tools and bits and pieces of the Indians' distinctive
pottery, which they decorated with the natural as-
phaltum found on the beach. In those calm backwaters
the Karankawas scavenged for clams and whelks;

they set up weirs and picked off the trapped fish with their longbows. At night, on spots such as these, they built driftwood bonfires and drank tea made from yaupon leaves that left them overstimulated and prey to visions.

The Karankawas, according to an early settler, were "the Ishmaelites of Texas, for their hands were against everyman and everyman's hand was against them." From Cabeza de Vaca onward, almost every white man who encountered those extraordinary people was struck by their exceptional height, by their expert skill as archers and canoeists, and finally by their absolute defiance of the new order. They had no use for horses and firearms, yet they fought the invading hordes with such skill and savagery that even such a mild-mannered soul as Stephen F. Austin ultimately found it necessary to call for their extermination.

In the end, that is what happened to them. No Karankawas exist today to give an accounting of themselves, and the folklore that has arisen about them has been filtered through hundreds of years of Anglo contempt. They are said to have been cannibals who enjoyed tying their victim to a stake, slicing off pieces of his flesh, and eating it before his eyes. One tall tale has them raiding villages and carrying off the children to eat as trail snacks on the journey back home. Another writer chastises them for their guttural language and even asserts that they had trouble pronouncing their own name.

So much about the Karankawas—their appearance, language, dress, weapons, attitude—was so strikingly different from other Texas Indians that they seem to have been an alien presence. One theory, espoused by Herman Smith, the staff archeologist at the Corpus Christi Museum, is that they were not North American Indians at all but Caribs from the West Indies who, sometime before Columbus, had made their way in dugout canoes from Antigua to the Texas coast.

The Caribs were the Vikings of the Caribbean, a ferocious, seagoing people who raided from island to island, who were tall and naked like the Karankawas, and who were such skilled swimmers and bowmen that they could loose arrows while treading water. Smith speaks of the Karankawa arrival in Texas as an invasion. "These guys came across Padre Island like John Wayne at Iwo Jima, and whatever other Indian groups were around then were flat out of business."

The Karankawas didn't stay in business that long either, but their presence on Padre was unerasable. Driving between a row of collapsed beach umbrellas and the seawall that guarded the Holiday Inn, I could feel some archaic power of place, an almost physical sensation that drifted across my skin like the blowing sand.

Surfers were gathered near an old wrecked fishing pier, looking out at the waves with their boards still in their cars, waiting for some promising sign before they committed themselves. One of the surfers had a parrot perched on his shoulder, and as I drove slowly by I overheard him telling a girl that the parrot did not just mimic words but could carry on an intelligent conversation in six languages.

Half a mile beyond, Bob Hall Pier protruded out into the surf on its concrete pilings. The original pier had been made of wood, and in my memory it was longer, so that in walking out to its end you could sense the choppy shallows giving way beneath your feet to the ocean deeps. I remembered hooking a large stingray out at the end of Bob Hall, and I could vividly recall the steady, unflinching pull of its wingbeats. The fish was not merely trying to get away; it was communicating its outrage, and when I saw its strange kite shape break the surface I felt as if I had committed some awful trespass against nature.

Hurricanes—Carla, Celia, Beulah, and finally Allen—had destroyed the old pier, and if the new structure was not quite as evocative, at least it appeared that it would last. The pier was part of what used to be called Nueces County Park. It had recently been named Padre Ballí Park, in deference to the priest from whom the whole island took its name. José Nicolás Ballí was the son of well-heeled Spanish colonists who had settled in the Rio Grande Valley in the late eighteenth century. His mother was a powerful and deeply religious woman who passed on to her son a facility for not drawing too fine a distinction between material and spiritual comforts. "Padre Ballí left," one modern author cheekily writes, "unmistakable evidence of a carnate existence."

Certainly the priest worked as hard at accruing capital as he did at saving souls. Sometime between 1800 and 1805 he applied to the crown for a grant to the unclaimed strip of land off the coast that Alonso Alvarez de Piñeda, searching for the Strait of Anian, had first named Isla Blanca. When his request was granted, he turned the island into a cattle ranch, placing his nephew in charge while he returned to the comforts of the mainland. The padre lived on the island only once, when he needed a refuge during the Mexican revolution of 1821, an event that assuredly did not favor the interests of an aristocratic Spanish priest. After the revolution, Ballí managed to reaffirm his original grant with the new government in Mexico, but he died soon after, leaving behind a succession of heirs whose hold on La Isla del Padre grew, over time, more and more tenuous.

I drove from Padre Ballí Park back onto the road that led down the center of the island to the national seashore. Soon the filling stations and beachwear emporiums gave way to the dunes and hummocky grasslands that covered the island between the beach and the laguna. Padre was wide here—two miles across—and the swaths of seacoast bluestem, unmarked by trees, looked limitless and pure.

The national seashore is 67.5 miles long, extending all the way to Mansfield Channel. It was created in 1962, after long and sometimes rancorous debate from private landowners and developers who were just beginning to realize the island's potential. A few miles from the entrance, the road I was traveling took a dogleg to Malaquite Beach, the park's only concession to the traditional beachgoer. Malaquite is half a mile long, a cultivated stretch of shoreline that is closed to automobile traffic.

The beach was almost deserted today. I went up to the big pavilion that housed a snack bar and bathhouses and looked out toward the Gulf, admiring the spotless sand and the wide expanse of blue water that began just outside the turbulent green of the surf. The snack bar was closed, as was the visitors' center, and the pavilion itself—only fifteen years old—was already an eerie relic, its concrete supports eaten away by the corrosive air.

From Malaquite on, there was no road at all. If you wanted to go farther, "down island," you had to have a vehicle that could pull you through the treacherous sand and shell banks that formed Padre's limitless beach. I drove the Blazer down to the waterline and pointed it south, planning to travel near the surf as long as the sand held firm.

Beyond Malaquite the beach was wide, and the shoreline slipped unobtrusively beneath the foamy, played-out waves that minutes before had broken with considerable power against the outer bar. The dunes were low and scruffy, fringed with waving sea oats and low-level creepers like fiddle-leaf morning glory. But between the beach and the dunes something was wrong. I kept thinking as I drove along that it could not possibly be this bad, but I was gradually forced to believe it. Padre Island National Seashore had, in the years since I had last ventured this far, become a vast trash heap.

Most of the garbage had been compressed by wave acton into one long strip, but it was difficult to find a square foot of beachfront that did not host an aluminum can or a beady chunk of Styrofoam. And it went on forever, a spectacle every bit as riveting as the natural vistas that I had driven down here to admire.

I was not naive. I was familiar enough with the island to understand that the pristine, undisturbed seashore it is advertised to have is largely a copywriter's dream. Because the middle section of Padre lies at the point of convergence of two longshore currents, it provides a continuous reading of the state of the Gulf. Things wash up here—shells, tree trunks, coconuts, rafts of sargassum, buoys, floats from fishing nets, bottles, even treasure. But the waves make no distinction between picturesque sea wrack and garbage, and the same forces that bring us doubloons and conch shells also deposit sopping mattresses and broken light bulbs.

Scattered along the beach that day, I later learned, were 142 tons of trash. The problem was most acute along the sixty miles of the national seashore. Only about four miles of beachfront are routinely kept clean, a job that falls to probationers from the U.S. District Court in Corpus Christi, who patrol the areas north and south of Malaquite Beach each week, picking up litter by hand. The National Park Service cannot begin to afford the cost of keeping the rest of the island clean, and so it is left to sink under the weight of a constant accumulation of bleach bottles, packing materials, egg cartons, bedsprings, and indissoluble plastics in an infinite variety of forms.

Island tourists are responsible for only a small percentage of the trash. The great majority comes from offshore—from oil and gas operations, from commercial shipping, and from the increasing pollution of the rivers that empty into the Gulf. Drop a paper cup into the Mississippi River in Hannibal, Missouri, in November, and it's likely to end up on Padre Island in January.

The laws governing ocean dumping are anemic. Most vessels in the Gulf of Mexico are restricted from tossing their garbage overboard only if they are inside three miles from shore, and even inside that narrow zone, it's easy enough for a crafty despoiler to evade the law.

I traveled on, with a heavy heart, in four-wheel drive. The corridor of trash and sargasso in the center of the beach was as unvarying as a traffic median. There were inordinate numbers of construction hard hats, rubber gloves, and the disembodied limbs of Third World baby dolls. Occasionally I would see a 55-gallon drum standing on end with a yellow sticker warning the curious not to approach. Such drums could be found all up and down the seashore. They were filled with solvents, antifreeze, drilling fluids containing dangerous heavy metals. They too came from the Gulf, from drilling platforms or passing ships—"moonlight dumpers." The National Park Service, at a price to the taxpayer of $1,000 per drum, periodically sent men in moon suits to remove them, identify their contents, and dispose of them.

So the two most dominant features of Padre Island were trash and toxic waste. It was enough to drive me to think about radical remedies—decommissioning the national seashore, for instance, and hoping that the resulting flood of demanding condo owners would see to it that the beach was kept clean. But that was a surly thought and only a cosmetic solution. No real change would come unless an enforceable ban on dumping could be extended far beyond the three-mile limit and ports were required to have waste-disposal facilities for ships that would otherwise dump their refuse at sea.

About fifteen miles past the park boundary, the composition of the beach began to change from sand to shell. This was Little Shell, a region whose surface was graded with fragments of coquina clams. The shell looked solid, but it shifted and gave way and provided uncertain footing for my vehicle's businesslike tires. The water washed over the shell in rounded cusps, and cormorants stood at the swash line on their heavy webbed feet, holding their wings out to dry. In the distant haze ahead I could see the island curving a bit, outward toward the Gulf.

At the fifteen-mile marker, near a giant fuel tank that was slowly oxidizing on the beach, I decided to make camp. There was a little draw where the dunes were blown out that looked like a good place, so I went to work clearing the site of garbage. When that was done I set up my new tent, which promptly took off into the air like a hang glider. Obviously, Sir Edmund Hillary had never camped on Padre Island. I was finally able to anchor it by setting six-gallon water jugs into the two windward corners.

That accomplished, I set off exploring. A pass had been dredged here several times in the forties and fifties as a way to regulate the salinity in the laguna, but the pass always closed in soon after it was finished, and now all that was left of it was a low, grassy valley that led through the dunes. A string of ponds followed the old course of the pass, and they were peopled with willets and shovelers and a little blue heron who loped ahead of me as I walked, hiding in the cattails until I flushed him out again.

Flies came to attack me. They were slow and easy to swat, but there was such an endless supply of them that I gave up my goal of walking to the other side of the island, a mile distant. Instead I climbed a high dune and looked out toward the laguna, which from that distance was merely a broad, shimmering mirage. A little to the south, in the center of the laguna, was a landmark called the Hole. The Hole was deep, and the water that surrounded it was so shallow that sometimes it would evaporate, leaving great numbers of fish swimming in a natural trap. Louis Rawalt, who spent most of his life on the island, described how on such occasions one person could take two or three thousand fish.

Rawalt came to the island in 1919 when he was 21. He had been gassed in World War I and was told not to expect to survive more than six months. He decided to live out his life on Padre, which he did, although he did not die until he was 82. He made a living by fishing and beachcombing, traveling up and down the island in his Model T. He once found a Mayan figurine that dated back to 4500 B.C. Another time, walking in the dunes, he came across the hull of a Spanish galleon.

As I walked back to my camp I remembered Rawalt's account of the day he had caught five hundred pounds of redfish while surf casting at Little Shell. I hadn't fished since high school, but I had brought along a rod and reel from those days; its monofilament line had turned as yellow as old newspaper. Why not give it a try? I got the rig out of the truck, clipped off the old leader, and put on a stainless steel hook and a fancy surf weight that would help keep my bait on the bottom, where the wily redfish prowled. The bait was dead shrimp. I remembered how to puncture them just under the rear fins—fragile as dragonfly wings—and let the hook travel through the body, bending the shrimp to its shape.

Now what? I waded out into the gut past the first bar. The water was not warm, and the waves were high enough to slam me in the chest and make me think about my footing. Standing on the next bar, I cast out ahead into the deeper water, trying to remember if this was the way you were supposed to do it. After five minutes I was looking at my watch. The body blows from the surf were not conducive to patience. Serious surf fishermen—I had passed a few of them on my way down—sat in lawn chairs and drank beer, their rods set into metal holders. But I had decided I would either do this like a sportsman or eat Sweet Sue Chicken 'n Dumplings for dinner after all.

Crabs were down there nibbling at my bait. They sent up delicate tremors through the brittle fishing line. After a while, because I was bored, I began to reel them in, admiring the tenacity with which they held onto the shrimp with one claw as they rose into the air.

Unable to recall a single instance in which I had actually caught a fish in the surf, I gave up and walked back to the truck and waited for night. When it came, moonless and chilly, I built a driftwood fire and watched the sparks, driven by the offshore wind, bound off into the dunes. They moved so swiftly that they seemed alive and willful, as if each glowing speck leapt out of the flames with a destination in mind.

The headlights of a jeep traveled down the beach. Its passage was marked as well by a regular series of percussive sounds—*pop-pop-pop*—as its tires hit the inflated sacs of beached Portuguese men-of-war. Except for the jeep, the beach was deserted. Offshore I counted nineteen lights. Half of them—the steady ones—were drilling platforms. The others were shrimp boats, trawling out beyond the bars where the shrimp were feeding in the dark water.

It was the sort of night that, long ago, would have appealed to those individuals who were in the business of wrecking and looting ships. Wreckers—some of whom were former pirates in the service of Jean Laffite—found the remote beaches and treacherous shoals of Padre Island to be a perfect location for their endeavors. They would typically attach a lantern to the end of a long pole that had been strapped to the front leg of a donkey, then lead the animal in tight circles on the beach. A captain at sea would read the distant, bobbing point of light as a buoy and steer his craft to the harbor he assumed it marked. By the time he realized his mistake, he would already have run aground on the outer bar.

The waters off Padre were dangerous enough, even without the services of wreckers, and hundreds of ships foundered there. One of the island's most notable castaways was John Singer, whose schooner, the *Alice Sadell*, broke apart in the surf in 1847. Singer and his wife, Johanna, built a shelter from the remains of the *Alice Sadell* and, while they waited for rescue, discovered that they liked the island well enough to stay.

Singer—whose brother was the inventor of the sewing machine—apparently had some capital, and over the years he built up a considerable ranching operation. At the site of Padre Ballí's old Rancho Santa Cruz, Singer constructed a house from mahogany timbers, a black-smith shop, and corrals. He and his wife had six children. When Johanna grew tired of island life, she put on a pair of canvas mittens and rowed a flat-bottomed skiff across the laguna and then traveled by oxcart to the relative splendor of Brownsville.

During the Civil War the island was part of the Confederate blockade. Because the Singers were openly pro-Union, they were forced off. In a panic they placed their fortune—$62,000 worth of jewelry and old Spanish coins—in a screw-top jar and buried it in the dunes. After the war they came back to the island to retrieve it, but it was the old story: the sands had shifted, the landmarks had disappeared, the treasure was lost. Singer searched for it for a year. His wife died. Finally he gave up and sailed for South America. Treasure hunters have been searching for Singer's ranch headquarters, the Lost City, ever since. A Brownsville man is said to have found it in 1931, but before he could locate the screw-top jar the sand had engulfed the site again.

WHEN THE FIRE DIED DOWN I TOOK A WALK ALONG the beach, the darkness so intense that I almost collided at one point with a giant cat's cradle of driftwood. I could not see the surf, but I could sense its movement, the constant crawl and slouch of the waves that could seem, from one moment to the next, either a

threat or a comfort. The sound of the waves was constant too, but I had long since stopped discerning it.
It was the aural baseline; above it was silence and, just
occasionally, the panicky whining of coyotes.

A friend to wildlife, I left some scraps out for the
coyotes and retired to the tent, listening to its fabric
snap and billow in the wind. The tent had a floor, so
I didn't worry about sand crabs, but sand drifted in
through the mesh windows, and I could feel it falling
on my face like pollen. I didn't mind. The air was
pleasantly rank—salt air—and I banished my outrage at
the despoiled beach and let my mind wander, coasting
into sleep on a childhood memory of bodysurfing,
recalling the sensation of soaring in those smooth
waves just before they broke.

By eight o'clock the next morning I had packed and
driven twenty miles farther down the beach to Big
Shell. The large cockleshells that covered the surface
of the beach were streaked with pale bands of color.
Unbroken sand dollars were everywhere, and dozens
of Portuguese men-of-war huddled together in one
spot, the wind having blown them all along the same
course. I took an inventory of the unnatural flotsam as
well. Within a five-foot radius of where I was standing
were a turquoise detergent bottle, a shredded egg carton, a bottle of Lea and Perrins sauce, a pair of light
blue Fruit of the Loom jockey shorts, a milk carton,
a plastic bag, a club soda bottle, three light bulbs, a
container of Lemon Pledge, a ski rope, a sandal, a
tuna can, three beer cans, a can of Puncture Seal, an
oil filter, and a carton of Acadia buttermilk from
Thibodaux, Louisiana.

I looked up in time to see an osprey dive deep into the surf and then shoot up like a subsurface missile, a mullet in its beak. A hundred yards down the beach a sea turtle was washing in. Its head was gone, and though the carcass was fresh enough to bleed, the flesh that was left was gruesome and moldy and hung like a tattered curtain covering the hole where the head had been. More than likely the turtle had been decapitated by a shrimper who had accidentally hauled it to the surface and wanted to ensure that it did no more damage to his nets.

The turtle's shell was about three feet in diameter. I took a good look at the arrangement of the scales on its plastron and then ran a make on it with my reptile book. It was a Kemp's ridley, a threatened species believed to have nested on Padre Island early in this century. Eight years ago a project had been started to reintroduce the turtles to the island. Eggs were collected from the ridleys' breeding ground in Mexico and buried in Padre Island sand. When the hatchlings emerged they were allowed to flap down the beach—thus imprinting the place on their consciousness—and then scooped out of the water. A year or so later, after growing to the size of saucers, they were tossed out into the Gulf. The hope was that their homing instincts would return them to Padre, but nobody would know, until the first hatchlings reached sexual maturity, if the project would succeed. Meanwhile, more and more turtles were washing up dead.

A high, conspicuous dune was nearby, blown out in the center like a volcanic crater. I wondered if it might be Black Hill, the site of one of the old line camps from Pat Dunn's ranch, but when I walked back into the dunes to investigate I could find no trace of the corral that was supposed to be still standing.

Pat Dunn—Don Patricio to his vaqueros—ran a cattle ranch on Padre Island for almost fifty years. He came out here with his two brothers in 1879, when he was 21 years old and the Kings and Kenedys were starting to put up fences on their vast mainland holdings. Forgotten and nearly inaccessible, Padre remained open range. It was in many ways an ideal location for a cattle ranch. Fresh water was available if one dug deep enough in the dunes, and the Gulf on one side and the laguna on the other served as natural boundaries. The narrow strip of land made the logistics of a roundup simple, and cattle were easy to spot in the almost treeless grass flats.

Dunn was thoroughly accommodated to island life. He built a home out of lumber found on the beach, furnishing it with chairs salvaged from a wrecked steamer. When a 125-pound tin of hardtack washed ashore he developed an unnatural fondness for its contents and hoarded it for years. He was kind to his cattle, preferring that his cowboys catch them by hand because he thought roping was cruel. The cattle in turn flourished, adapting to the island so completely that Don Patricio called them "sea lions." They licked dead fish for salt and wallowed in the asphalt deposits and supposedly ate crabs off the beach. To get them to market they had to be swum across the laguna, and from such peculiar trail drives there grew persistent stories of drovers lassoing redfish.

Over the years Dunn acquired title to almost all of

Padre Island, selling it in 1926 for $125,000 to Colonel Sam Robertson, who dreamed of turning it into a major resort until a hurricane blew away his improvements. Dunn moved to Corpus Christi. He maintained a suite in the Driscoll Hotel and was driven around by a chauffeur, but he seemed less content than in the years when he nibbled hardtack on Padre Island.

"If the Lord would give me back the island now," he groused after he sold out, "wash out a channel in Corpus Christi Pass thirty feet deep, and put devilfish and other monsters in it to keep out the tourists, I'd be satisfied."

A SHRIMP BOAT WAS AGROUND ON THE BEACH AT the thirty-mile marker. Its name was the *Majestic Clipper*, and it was canted to one side, its port outrigger dipping into the surf. The *Majestic Clipper* was a large seagoing vessel, maybe eighty feet long, and on the otherwise featureless shoreline it took on scale, so that it seemed to have the dimensions of an ocean liner.

While I was inspecting the boat, a man looked down from the bow, tossed a rope over the side, and shimmied barefoot down to the sand.

"Hola," he said when he landed. He told me he was from Brownsville and was the only member of the crew still aboard. Everyone else had left the day the *Majestic Clipper* tangled a line in its prop and ran aground. But the captain had ordered him to stay on board so that nobody could claim salvage rights. That had been nineteen days ago, he said, in a tone that implied it was no fun to be a castaway. For one

thing, it was hard to sleep in a boat that was tilted at a 45-degree angle.

He stood back, peeling an orange that I had given him, and looked at the boat as if he were studying his predicament for the first time. "Maybe the captain will come this week," he said, then shrugged. "Maybe not."

I left the shrimper some more fruit and drove on, reminded anew of Padre's reputation as the graveyard of the Gulf. The history of the island is in large part the history of shipwreck, and the evidence of its fatal magnetism is never far from sight. Some miles past the *Majestic Clipper* were the ruins of the *Nicaragua,* a coastal steamer that was driven aground during a storm in 1912. The rusted boilers of the ship rose prominently from the surf, their presence tampering with the normal course of the waves and causing a surge that periodically left one or two other jagged hulks of steel exposed.

Ten miles beyond the *Nicaragua* were the granite jetties of Mansfield Channel. A truck chassis had sub-sided into the sand at the edge of the boulders, and a pile of soft drink cans had been effectively sandblasted by the high winds until their labels were effaced and they shone like a precious metal. I climbed onto the jetties and walked out fifty yards or so, watching the sea lice scatter around the boulders and listening to the suction of the water in the crevices below. Mansfield Channel, built in the late fifties to provide the main-land village of Port Mansfield with access to the Gulf, was the terminus of the national seashore, though Padre Island itself ran for another forty miles on the

other side. The channel was wide, and the water here
was blue. A shrimp boat, flying the skull and cross-
bones, was moving through the jetties out to the Gulf,
its wake disturbing a small sportfishing boat, *Yesterday's
Wine*, that was anchored near the channel marker.

A terrible thing happened here in 1554. Of all the
shipwrecks that have occurred on Padre Island, the
loss of the Spanish treasure fleet is the most lurid and
unforgettable, the event that forever fixed the island's
reputation as a savage and alluring place.

"Woe to those of us who are going to Spain, because
neither we nor the fleet will arrive there," a Spanish
priest named Juan Ferrer is said to have proclaimed as
his ship left Veracruz. "Most of us will perish, and
those who are left will experience great torment,
though all will die in the end except a very few."

Such dire predictions were not out of character for
Fray Ferrer, who was so full of strange and cryptic
pronouncements that he had been summoned back to
Spain by the emperor to "give an account of his
dreams and fantasies." His fellow passengers were
noblemen and merchants who were sailing home with
their families, bearing the fortunes they had made in
New Spain. The four ships that sailed from Veracruz
were heavily laden as well with the crown's revenue
from the enterprises of its colony. *Santa María de
Yciar*, the only ship whose register still exists, carried
more than 15,000 pounds of silver, most of it in coins
stored in casks.

The ships were to sail to Havana, where they would
join a larger fleet for protection in the Atlantic crossing. But twenty days out of port they were struck by

a violent spring storm. One of the ships managed to make it to Havana, but the other three, running before the storm, were blown all the way back across the Gulf and broke apart within a few miles of each other on the shore of Padre Island.

About three hundred Spaniards, many of them women and children, survived the wrecks. For reasons that are unclear, they decided to abandon the shelter and provisions that could have been salvaged from the ships and undertake a march to the Spanish settlement of Pánuco, which they thought lay two or three days to the south. What lay between them and Pánuco, however, was not only the whole southern half of Padre Island but three hundred miles of marshy coastal lands on the other side of the Rio Grande. For seven days they walked south under the open sun, eating what shellfish they could find and licking the leaves of plants for moisture, unaware that they could find fresh water by digging in the dunes.

Finally they were approached by about a hundred Indians (likely Karankawas) who offered the Spaniards food and then stood by suspiciously as they ate. It dawned on the castaways that they were trapped, and as the Indians watched they began quietly to prepare themselves, readying the two crossbows and various other weapons that they had salvaged from the wreck. When their hosts attacked they were able to repulse them, but as they continued their march the Indians dogged their steps, picking off stragglers with their bows and arrows.

In twelve days they reached the Rio Grande. Crossing the river on makeshift rafts, they lost their crossbows. Soon after, two Spaniards were captured by the Indians and then released when they had been stripped of their clothes. That incident gave the castaways hope that all the Indians wanted was their garments, and in desperation they took off their clothes and cast them on the sand.

Naked, debased, defenseless, the Spaniards marched on. The priests sent the unclothed women in advance, where the men could not see them. One chronicler reports that some of the women dropped dead from shame.

When the women and children reached the Rio de las Palmas they barely had time to drink before the Indians attacked, shooting from a distance with their powerful bows. "The wounded child would run toward the mother for help," we are told, "but the wound was felt by the mother as if it were her own."

By the time the men came upon the scene, all of the women and children were dead. The men walked on, two hundred of them. On the other side of the river fifty of them were killed. The remainder walked for twenty more days, picked off one by one until their hopeless trek to Pánuco ended in annihilation.

There were two survivors. A priest named Fray Marcos de Mena, left for dead in the dunes after being struck with seven arrows, somehow revived enough to continue the journey. He went for four days without food or water, and when he collapsed at night sand crabs picked at his wounds. Muttering prayers as the staggered down the beach, he finally reached Pánuco. The other survivor, a soldier named Francisco Vásquez, broke off from his companions and walked alone

back to the wreck site. He was there only a few days
before he was rescued by the salvage fleet that had
been hastily organized once word of the loss of the
treasure ships reached Veracruz.

The salvage crew set up a camp on Padre Island,
and for months divers, using only lung power, brought
up load after load of silver *reales*. At the end of the
project, only half the treasure had been recovered.
The rest sank into the sand bottom, along with the
ships' timbers and fittings and the personal effects of
the doomed passengers.

For four hundred years silver coins have been washing up on the beach north of Mansfield Channel.
When the channel was made, the dredge passed right
through the final resting place of the *Santa María de
Yciar*, destroying the site but bringing to the surface,
among other relics, one of the ship's anchors.

Such discoveries narrowed the field of search for
treasure hunters, and in 1967 a salvage firm from Indiana located the wreck of the *Espíritu Santo* and began
hauling up artifacts. The search was promptly shut
down by Jerry Sadler, the Texas land commissioner,
who argued that the treasure belonged to "the school-
children of Texas." A long-running legal contest sent
the salvage firm back to Indiana, and the state, in the
guise of the newly formed Texas Antiquities Committee, moved in to claim its prize. In the early seventies
the committee launched a full-scale underwater archeology project, burrowing through the sea bottom
to find anchors, astrolabes, fragments of timber, verso
cannon, and crucifixes.

And of course treasure. The archeologists brought
up bullion disks and gold bars and hundreds of silver

coins, but when the project was over a great deal more
was left buried in the sand. Under the antiquities law
all of it belongs to the state. Pocketing anything—
coins, cannonballs, corroded spikes—is a crime pun-
ishable by a fine of up to $1,000 and a jail term of
up to thirty days.

"Treasure is there for all, for you and you and you,"
writes one splenetic author. "But now, in the event
you do manage to unearth one of these fast-eroding
coins . . . YOU ARE REQUIRED BY LAW to take it to
someone sitting in their air-conditioned office and
GIVE it to them."

Treasure hunters still converge on Padre, despite
the antiquities law and despite the certainty that their
metal detectors will be confiscated if discovered by a
park ranger. "If you find anybody camped two miles
north of the jetties," a treasure hunter named Dave
told me, "I can guarantee you, they're hunting."

I had met Dave at a hotel bar in Corpus. The meeting had been arranged by intermediaries, as carefully
as if it were to be a meeting with a mob boss instead
of an outlaw hobbyist.

"My position is this," he said. "Once you establish
the historical significance of a site and the kinds of
finds that are going to be made, why not go ahead and
let people find the relics? The archeologists don't have
any use for these coins. They're not going to tell them
anything they don't already know.

"I don't feel like a criminal, but the first couple of
times I went down there I was scared the whole time.
I've seen people get so worried they make themselves
sick to their stomachs."

Dave hunts mostly in the winter, after high tides or

storms. He drives down in the daytime, sets up camp, and hunts all night, sweeping his metal detector over the sand and illuminating his way with a single flashlight. If he sees a car coming or anything suspicious he turns off the light and hides the detector in the dunes. He has never been caught, and he knows of only one person who has been arrested on Padre Island since the antiquities law went into effect. Even so, he's paranoid.

He looked around warily and took out of his jeans pocket several plastic bags containing coins he'd found on the beach. The silver pieces were dark gray, their edges ragged and worn thin. They were coins from the 1554 shipwrecks, minted in Mexico City in denominations of 2 and 4 *reales*. The names of Carlos and Johanna, the rulers of the Holy Roman Empire, were imprinted in a circle around a rendering of the pillars of Hercules. "Usually when you find a coin," he said, with a glance at a passing waiter who seemed a little too interested in our conversation, "there'll be so much tar and debris on it, it'll look just like a piece of tar."

Dave said that he finds coins, usually a few a night, on two out of three trips down to the island. In the last six years about two thousand coins from the 1554 wrecks have been found on the beach by treasure hunters. Almost all of them have been in denominations of 2 or 4 *reales*. A few 3-*real* pieces have been found, but they're very rare. One of those, in good condition, might sell for $600.

"Back in the fifties and sixties there were some people who supposedly made a lot of money digging up coins off the island and selling them in Mexico, but it's not really profitable anymore. I wouldn't ever sell any of these coins anyway. One day, I suppose, I'll put them in a museum somewhere."

I picked up one of the coins and ran my finger along its worn surface, thinking about how this blackened, wafer-thin object had once been part of the wealth of New Spain. Now, four centuries since its loss, it was something considerably less than a piece of treasure and more than a souvenir.

Today, walking by the jetties, I scanned the ground ahead, almost unconsciously looking for a flat disk of tar that might hide such a coin. I found nothing, of course, which was probably for the best, because in my heart I was not sure I would be able to obey the antiquities law that forbade me to touch it.

MANSFIELD CHANNEL WAS A MAJOR OBSTACLE IN MY journey down the island. There was no bridge or ferry to take me across, and swimming or hitching a ride on a boat would have meant leaving the Blazer behind. I thought about how formidable this body of water must seem to the illegal aliens who use the island as a route north from Mexico. They have to cross the deep pass clinging to inner tubes.

The only feasible way for me to get to the other side was to drive back to Corpus, fly to South Padre Island, and then proceed northward on the island until I reached the opposite shore. A week later that was where I was, sitting across the channel on the jetties, eating lunch and watching a pod of dolphins in the pass. They were feeding in a school of mullet, close enough to where I was sitting that every so often one of them would raise an eye above the waterline and look at me.

From that point south, the island was privately owned, but there was little to distinguish it from the national seashore until one reached the condominium towers of South Padre Island. There was no road on this part of the island either, so I had rented a three-wheel all-terrain vehicle and driven up from South Padre on the beach.

The ATV had been more fun than I had expected, and as I sat on the jetties, studiously observing the dolphins eating their mullet, I could not keep my eyes from the bright yellow vehicle parked on the beach. Soon I was roaring off again down the swash line, popping men-of-war with my knobby tires and leaping over piles of sargassum. Ghost crabs, their eye stalks fully extended in alarm, zipped into their burrows at my approach.

Except for a few more drums of toxic waste, the trash problem on this side of the island was not as severe, and the wide beach grew cleaner and the water clearer the farther south I headed. Over by the low, unsecured dunes the sand was surprisingly firm. Coyote tracks were imprinted there, and the ripple marks the wind had made in the tightly packed sand reminded me of the dense cloud patterns of a mackerel sky.

The island was narrower here, and the dune fields were more likely to be breached by hurricane passes. I veered off into the mouth of one pass, opening my machine up all the way on the hypnotic flats. The laguna was no more than a mile and half away, but the landscape was so featureless that the distance seemed infinite. I passed over the flats at full throttle, in a kind of dream state, like a person falling through the air. I picked up the tracks of some cloven-footed animal—a javelina, probably—followed them to the edge of the dunes, and then took off into the open again, down-shifting as the sand became softer toward the far side of the island.

I had heard stories of vehicles such as mine dropping out of sight into deep beds of quicksand out on the flats. I wasn't convinced that the stories were true, but as I drew closer to the laguna, I paid particular attention to the consistency of the sand, worried that I might suddenly hear a slurping sound and find that it was all over. The bare flats were decorated with shell now, and there were a few isolated hillocks of back-island dunes. A carpet of blanched sea grass bordered the waterline, and a flotilla of little pink bryozoans was just drifting into shore. I waded out into the shallow water, not much liking the feel of the ooze beneath my feet, and looked without success for snail tracks. A formless, wraithlike creature, maybe an inch across, moved with surprising speed just beneath the surface, but I lost it when I took another step and clouded up the water.

Standing in the laguna, I was on the property of the State of Texas. In 1940 Texas had pressed a claim to the island itself, contending that the original Ballí grant was invalid. The suit was titled *State of Texas* v. *Ballí et al.*, and even though the state lost the suit and the Ballí grant was affirmed, it was the et als, not the Ballís, who carried the day. The padre's descendants had, practically speaking, long ago lost ownership to people like Pat Dunn, who moved onto the island and acquired title by right of possession.

The defendants in the Ballí case included real estate developers and land speculators, people who had a stake in bringing to reality the long-cherished fantasy of turning Padre Island into the Gold Coast of Texas. With the state's claim denied, there was nothing to stand in the way of the boom.

But the state did derive some benefit from the suit. It managed to set the western boundary of the island according to a survey conducted by J. Stuart Boyles. The Boyles line was more or less consistent with the observable shoreline, and so it left almost the whole of the Laguna Madre—and its potential for oil and gas revenue—in the possession of Texas.

Private owners have been sniping at the Boyles line ever since in an effort to extend their title westward into the laguna. In 1969 they commissioned another survey, by M. L. Claunch, that concluded that the mean high water line of the Laguna Madre was considerably westward of the place where Boyles put it. In 1980 a group of developers sued the state, claiming ownership of a part of the submerged land between the Boyles and Claunch lines. The state, wanting to avoid the expense of a lengthy trial, gave in, a position it has since regretted. Nowadays at the General Land Office the Boyles line is regarded as a sacred boundary. If it is breached further, they say, Texas could lose half of the laguna.

Padre Island's boundaries have always been elusive, its ownership always vague. It has been a difficult place to grasp with any instrument other than the imagination. No doubt I was trespassing on some-body's land as I made my way back to the public beach easement, but I gunned my ATV without remorse. The island was vacant and still, and there was a certain natural primacy in just being here. I liked the way that Padre Ballí had originally taken possession. He had picked up rocks and thrown them in the four direc-tions, and then bent down and drunk the water of the Laguna Madre. Those were gestures that seemed designed not to appease the bureaucrats of Spain but to appease, in some way, the island itself.

Ten miles down the island, the beach narrowed to a strip of sand guarded by a high balustrade of dunes. The dunes formed a series of peaks, a miniature mountain range rising thirty feet into the air. On the highest peak someone had planted a cross made of driftwood, and when I climbed up to inspect it and saw the view from that spot, I felt light-headed with appreciation. On one side was the abbreviated beach and the green Gulf water, so transparent that I could see a shoal of fish beneath its surface, an oscillating blue circle that swept slowly northward. The inland side was protected by dunes. The greenery began at the summit where I was standing and swept down-ward in a series of swales that ran all the way to the gleaming whiteness of the tidal flats. The carpet was broken only by several small ponds, brackish and short-lived, that nevertheless appeared as deep and cold as glacier lakes.

I had no idea if the cross was there merely to mark the view or if had some deeper significance. The view was enough, though. This was the spot. I suppose I believed at that moment that Padre Island was, in some unfathomable fashion, alive and aware, and that this was its pulse.

But there's nothing like a ride on an ATV to clear your head of mysticism, and soon I was yahooing down the beach again. In the haze ahead loomed the fabled city of South Padre Island, and as I entered its jurisdiction I observed the speed limit and adjusted my attitude. I was here just after spring break and a few weeks before the summer tourist season, and so the place had a downtime feel—not appealingly logy like a genuine coastal town, just a shade vacant and re-mote. Its buildings—its Bahia Mars and Canta Mars, its Windsongs and Bali Hais—rose upward in some-times shocking vertical counterpoint to the low-lying sandbar that supported them. I could almost feel the island sinking under their weight.

Thirty years ago South Padre had been little more than a Coast Guard station and a collection of fishing huts. Now, in full flower, it had the feeling of a city that had come up too fast. And yet I always found it a hard place not to like. Perhaps I was just a sucker for its furious fun-in-the-sun mores. Across the laguna sat Port Isabel, with its shrimp fleet, its hardware stores, its Union Carbide plant, as if South Padre had willfully shoved all the grimy and workaday demands of existence onto the mainland. It clearly preferred the role of grasshopper to Port Isabel's ant.

I CHECKED INTO A ROOM AT THE HILTON AND walked out onto the beach to sample the aquaculture.

It was a clean stretch of sand that recorded the footprints of joggers and the tracks of the big graders that
swept up and down the beach removing garbage.
Dunes were struggling to be born in the gaps between
the high rises, but elsewhere the familiar island zones
had been obliterated and there was only the gorgeous,
foreshortened beach.

Lying there, I read more lurid accounts of Karankawa cannibalism. "In this manner," the author of my
book noted, "the Indian tribes would kill the survivors
for food. Instead of shopping at the supermarket, they
did their food shopping in this manner."

I digested a few more pages of such lore and then
ventured into the surf. The firm sand at the waterline
was nearly free of shells, and the shore dropped off
cleanly. Past the second bar I was already over my
head. The waves formed and broke elegantly, and I
was struck by how much more comfortable I felt than
I usually did in Padre surf. There was nothing here: no
Portuguese men-of-war, no seaweed, no strange drifting blobs tickling the hair on my legs. I floated on my
back, my eyes closed, relaxing even my perpetual
vigilance of sharks. There was no menace in this water
or even any inconvenience. But I surprised myself by
missing the trash-strewn beach north of here, where
the trash itself now seemed like an index of wildness,
of the island's unruly and unprotected essence.

THE NEXT DAY I JOINED UP WITH A GROUP OF
travel writers who were being wooed by the South
Padre Island Tourist Bureau. We went for a morning
cruise in the Laguna Madre and then boarded a bus for

a look at a new condo that Ben Barnes and John Connally had built in the center of town. The building was called the Sunchase. Its two gleaming white towers, each a halved pyramid, rose up and up into the Padre Island sky, suggesting, we were told, a bird in flight. The towers were crowned by twin penthouses. "Obviously," our guide said as we filtered into the south penthouse, "Mr. Barnes and Mr. Connally think this will be the next Miami Beach of the Southwest."

The penthouse was unfurnished, as stark and correct as an art museum. It had recently been sold for about $700,000. The Sunchase straddled the island in such a way that from any one of the penthouse's deep windows or balconies you could see both the Gulf and the laguna. The island beneath us was such a narrow, feeble thing that I felt like a sailor in a crow's nest looking down at the deck of his ship.

"The amenities here," the guide informed us, "include a dry sauna, a steambath, racquetball, and tennis. In addition to this building, last year we started Sunchase Mall. We think this will be a nice amenity for this building and a nice amenity for South Padre Island in general. We hope there will be some nice restaurants there, and that will be a further amenity."

It became clear as our tour of South Padre Island progressed that the whole city was in itself a gigantic amenity, a way to make this unforgiving sandbar not only habitable but luxurious. In a curious way the city was distancing itself from the island, building up and away from it instead of embracing it. The island was more and more peripheral to the great free-floating resort colony it had spawned.

Next we went to see the Turtle Lady. "Now, she's not a crazy lady who dresses turtles up in clothes," our tour leader told us as we began to file out of the bus. "Well, she *does* dress her turtles up in clothes, but that's just for the small children, to keep them interested."

The Turtle Lady's real name was Ila Loetscher. She lived in a house on Gulf Boulevard whose foyer was dominated by wooden troughs filled with circulating seawater in which maimed sea turtles swam about. The Turtle Lady wore a white blouse with puffy sleeves under a black vest that said "Save the Ridleys." Her goal in life, she explained breathlessly, was to make the world safe for Kemp's ridleys like the one I had seen washed up on Big Shell.

Her means of raising consciousness on that matter was, to say the least, peculiar. From one of the troughs she picked up a turtle the size of a serving platter and held him upright in front of her. "His name is Lynn," she said, "and he wants to say hello."

The turtle flapped his front flippers.

"What do you do, honey," she asked him, "when you want to be kissed?"

Lynn laid his head back in a languid manner. The Turtle Lady kissed him on his bony beak.

"It only took me a week to train this little child to do that," she said. "You give him love first, and he will knock himself out trying to please you."

She held the turtle out to us. "Anybody else want to kiss him?"

When we demurred, she led us out into the back yard, where larger turtles—ridleys and greens and hawksbills—were kept in concrete tanks. Several of the turtles were missing flippers. Another had been brought to the Turtle Lady in a coma after he had eaten fish coated with tar.

"They are very loving little creatures," she said, gazing blissfully into the tank. "Every night these two go to that corner together and put their flippers around each other. So I know they dearly love each other. Of course they dearly love us too."

She picked up a female turtle she called Dave Irene and said, "Okay, let's play our game." The Turtle Lady pretended to chew on the turtle's flipper, then began smooching her on the neck, smearing lipstick on the creature's white wattly skin. "She could play this game all day long," the Turtle Lady said, though Dave Irene's reactions were not noteworthy. It is difficult for a sea turtle to look any way but indifferent.

On the way out I sneaked a peak in a downstairs closet. There, on hangers, was a row of frilly dresses in infant sizes. Turtle clothes. There were tiny sombreros too, and tiny little beds.

In the background I could hear the Turtle Lady cooing. "That's right," she said. "Uh huh. You're Mama's little baby, aren't you?"

DRIVING AROUND TOWN LATER ON MY OWN, I NOticed a statue of Padre Ballí that faced the incoming traffic on the Queen Isabella Causeway. When I asked how it had gotten there, I was told to talk to Johnny Ballí.

Johnny Ballí is Juan Jose Ballí, a great-grandnephew of the padre and a resident of Brownsville, where he is a border inspector for the Alcoholic Beverage Commission.

"It took five years of my life to get that statue up," he told me over a Whataburger in Port Isabel. "But it was worth it. When I was going to school I remember telling my teachers in history class that I came from the family that owned the island. I was always laughed at. Now my nieces and nephews can get up in history class and say, 'My family once owned this island, and there's a statue to prove it.' "

Ballí had wanted to meet in Port Isabel rather than South Padre because he didn't like the idea of spending money in establishments that were effectively fleecing him of his inheritance. "This is a family," he said, "that got a royal grant, and then we got a royal screw. It burns my ass to know that other people are enjoying something that doesn't belong to them. It's our birthright—it's ours!

"You'll have to excuse me if I get angry when I talk about this. I tend to get a little excited. But I'm not running in a popularity contest here. If somebody gets pissed off, piss on 'em!"

Just exactly what happened to the Ballís' hold on Padre Island is unclear. *State of Texas* v. *Ballí* proved the validity of the original Spanish grant, but long before that the waters had been muddied. Non-Ballís had been buying and selling the island for generations, and if today's descendants of those usurpers did not have an unsullied claim, they had something more powerful on their side: reality.

Just thinking about the way things had turned out made Johnny Ballí squirm in his booth in outrage. But if he hadn't gotten his family's land back, he had been remarkably successful in making sure that nobody around ever forgot the name "Ballí." In 1977 he fired his first salvo by standing up at a Cameron County commissioners' meeting and announcing that as a member of the Ballí family he was claiming possession of Padre Island. For five years he haunted the courthouse, lobbying for a statue of his ancestor. He rallied other members of the family. Two hundred strong, they once marched to Padre from Brownsville. Another time a group of militant Ballí heirs blocked off the causeway leading to their ancestor's island. In 1981 Johnny Ballí won his battle for the statue. Cameron County spent $40,000 to appease the Ballís, although Johnny is miffed that few of the dignitaries invited to the unveiling bothered to show up.

"It's like standing at a bakery window," Johnny said, "just looking outside. Look what I'm bucking, man—people like John Connally. Big John himself. But maybe if I became filthy rich he could become my buddy. I know how to spend a million dollars just as well as the next guy. Hell, I've got good taste!"

We drove back over the causeway to look at the statue. The padre stood with his arms outstretched, a crucifix in his right hand. He was saying, according to Johnny, "Welcome to my island."

"The greatest moment in my life was the day my father saw that statue," Johnny said. "When it arrived here from Italy, they took us out to the warehouse to see it. It was up high in a big crate, and they had us get on a forklift so they could lift us up to see his face. My dad, he couldn't believe it. He saw it and he just broke down and cried."

PADRE ISLAND ENDED A MILE OR SO SOUTH OF THE statue. Just past the causeway, at the Cameron County line, the resort glamour of South Padre began to trail off. Here there were water slides, video parlors, camp-sites of crushed shell where forlorn little pup tents were sandwiched between duded-up RVs. Widow's walks made of salt-stained lumber had been attached to the tops of some of the mobile homes in Isla Blanca Park, and as I drove along I could hear the barking of seals from a nearby mom-and-pop oceanarium.

I got out and walked along the jetties that guarded Brazos Santiago Pass. Nearby, in an almost empty pavilion, a band was playing in competition with the tape decks from the cars parked on the access road. High school kids promenaded from car to car, a be-havioral logic as deeply encoded as that of the ruddy turnstones that were scavenging among the jetties for crabs.

I looked north, up the island that was Johnny Ballí's birthright. The view was not all that good—there was the steady pressure of development on this end, the scandalous state of the beach on the national seashore. I counted on Padre Island to withstand those abuses, not knowing if it could. It seemed strange to me that this insubstantial sandbar could have had such a con-stant, lifelong hold on my imagination. Watching the mild waves slide onto the beach, I felt inarticulate, subdued—ready, like that ancient priest, to cast rocks to the four winds, to drink the water of the laguna, and claim the island as my own.

WHAT TEXAS
MEANS TO ME

LYING IN A FEATHER BED, IN THE GUEST ROOM OF a friend's two-hundred-year-old house in western Massachusetts, I suffered a lapse of faith in Texas. I'm not sure what brought this crisis on. Perhaps it was simply the act of waking up, looking out the window at the syrup buckets hanging from the maple trunks, at the banked snow glistening in the sharp air, and realizing that Texas would never be that.

I could stand to live here, I thought. I would keep my cross-country skis propped by the front door, a bowl of apples on the kitchen table, a steady fire by which I would read during the dim winter nights.

But it was not just Massachusetts. The hard truth was that I was getting tired of Texas and was now able to imagine myself living in all sorts of places: on one of those minor Florida keys where a little strip of land containing a shopping center and a few houses counted as barely a riffle in a great sheet of translucent ocean; in an adobe house, even a fake adobe house, in the foothills of the Sangre de Cristos; or perhaps in a city like Los Angeles, which with its corrupted natural beauty seemed so much more likely a center for the development of urban chaos than Houston.

These were uneasy rumblings, and I was enough of a Texan to feel heretical in even allowing them access to my conscious mind. But my affection for Texas had gone unexamined and untested for so long that it was time to wonder just how much affection was there after all. There are certain people who are compelled to live in Texas, but I was never one of them. I am not a two-fisted free enterpriser, I have no fortune to make in the next boom, and my ancestral ties to the land itself are casual and desultory. Like a lot of other Texans, I am here because I am here, out of habit, out of inertia, out of a love of place that I want to believe is real and not just wished for.

Because I was born in Oklahoma and lived there until I was five, I missed being imprinted with native fealty for Texas. I don't recall having any particular image of the state when, on the occasion of my widowed mother's marriage to an Abilene oilman, I was told we were going to move there. But I did not much care to leave Oklahoma City, where my baby footprints were embedded in cement and where the world of permanence and order was centered. In the park behind our house was a sandstone boulder where several generations of children had scratched their initials. This boulder, whose markings seemed to me to have some ancient significance, like the markings on a rune stone, was one of my power centers, one of the things that persuaded me that I had not been placed arbitrarily on the earth but was meant to exist here, at this particular spot. In the same park was a little garden with a semicircular rock wall dominated by a bust of Shakespeare and brass plaques containing quotations from his plays. It was a place to ponder and reflect on the immortal bard, but its hushed and reverent aspect made me mistake it for a tomb. I had no real idea who Shakespeare was, only that he was one of those exalted characters like Will Rogers, and so it seemed perfectly appropriate to me that he would be buried in Oklahoma.

But all such reverberations stopped at the Red River. I filed them away, and with a child's tenacity I resisted letting Texas invade my essence. Abilene, Texas, had been named for Abilene, Kansas, and that fact was a convincing enough argument that it would be a dull and derivative place. Our house there had a dry, nappy lawn and a cinder-block fence. My brother and I attended a Catholic school that, in this West Texas stronghold of stark and bilious religions, was like a foreign mission. On feast days the nuns would show us western movies and serve us corn dogs. Nearby there was a dispiriting lake where drab water lapped at a caliche shoreline, and on the southern horizon were low hills—looking on a map now, I see they are called the Callahan Divide—that I longed to think of as mountains.

But I surprised myself by being happy there. I liked the excitement of being rousted from sleep on summer evenings and taken to a neighbor's storm cellar to wait out a tornado warning. Though I did not know what an oilman was exactly, I enjoyed visiting my new father's office, looking at the charts and drilling logs and playing with the lead dinosaurs on his desk.

"Well, they sure do grow 'em tall down there in Texas," my relatives in Oklahoma would say when we went back to visit, and I began to imagine they were right and to cultivate a little my Texan identity. In my heart I knew that I lived in Anywhere, USA, that I watched *Crusader Rabbit* after school just like the kids in Winnemucca, and that my image of my own environment came from the same sources that everyone else's did: from *Giant*, from *Davy Crockett*, from a thousand stray pieces of folklore and merchandising.

But even this stitched-together notion of Texas had its power. Everybody else seemed to believe that Texas children were out there on the raw frontier, riding horses to school and pumping oil in the back yard, so who was to blame for us believing it a little ourselves? Even the false image provided a certain pride of place and left one more open for the real but impalpable expressions of the land itself. It became easier to imagine that the trim suburban streets down which I teetered uneasily on my first bicycle had been the setting for trail drives and Comanche raids. And there were other times when the land was almost unbearably evocative. Riding home at night from one of those Oklahoma trips, with the windows open, the car smelling of spoiled fruit, and the seats strewn with comic books and cracker crumbs, I would allow myself to become hypnotized by the way the headlights illuminated the barbed wire and mesquite on the sides of the road, creating a corridor, an endless bower that led us on but seemed never to deliver us into the land's ghostly heart. And then we would hit some little nothing town and the headlights would fall on the bobbing pump jacks, whose rhythms were keyed to a languid, eternal pulse that seemed to be everywhere, in the swooping wingbeats of nocturnal birds crossing the road, in the pistons of the car, and in my own heavy blood.

"I can see Abilene," my father would say when we were still fifty miles from home. "I can see a fly sitting on the window of our house."

"Where?" I would say, peering hard through the windshield, believing it was possible to see that far, as far as Texas went.

WHEN I WAS TEN WE MOVED TO CORPUS CHRISTI and I found that the image of Texas I had been cultivating and was now at ease with did not apply to this semi-exotic coastal city with its manicured bay front. This was not cowboy land. It was a sultry, complicated place, although the agoraphobia induced by the stillness of the ocean was reminiscent at times of the West Texas plains.

For my first six months there I was virtually felled by the humidity. I moved about in a tentative, purposeless way, like the anole lizards that wandered around the yard.

It was not a seductive place, but once you had purged your mind of false expectations and your pores of the last lingering traces of dry West Texas air, you began to feel accepted and absorbed by it. And of course Corpus Christi had its traditional charms as well—beaches and such—that the people at the tourist bureau seized every opportunity to promote. They kept shoving into the public view Buccaneer queens and Miss Naval Air Stations, who posed seductively among the sailboat rigging for brochures that advertised "The Sparkling City by the Sea."

A ten-year-old boy could tell they were trying too hard, but I secretly wished the boosters luck. Corpus seemed isolated not only from the world at large but from the conventional stereotypes of Texas. It was not until the TV show *Route 66* deigned to film an episode there that I felt I had been provided with convincing evidence that the city was real.

I remember going to the courthouse one day to watch the filming of a scene. Within sight of this spot, Alonso de Piñeda had passed on his great reconnaissance cruise in 1519. On this bay shore Zachary Taylor had brought in 1845 nearly half of the United States Army and encamped while waiting to provoke a war with Mexico. On this very spot, perhaps, stood the makeshift stage on which Lieutenant Ulysses S. Grant had played Desdemona during a production in that camp of *Othello*. I was ignorant of all that, but there on the courthouse steps strode Martin Milner, and it was as if the shadow of history had passed across me.

There were not many moments like that, and the study of Texas history in the seventh grade served only to confirm my suspicion that the state seemed somewhere to have gone flat. Texas history began with Indians, conquistadores, pirates, with revolutions and wars, but by the time the student reached "Texas Today and Tomorrow" in the history book he saw only pictures of sorghum fields, refineries, and official portraits of dowdy governors.

So as time wore on and the universal ill humors of adolescence began to work their magic, I slid deeper into the down cycle of what I fear may turn out to be a lifelong mood swing about Texas. Corpus especially rankled and galled me. As a college-bound high school graduate, I had a clear shot at leaving Texas for good, but when it came down to actually making a decision about where I was going to go to school I threw in with thousands of other freshmen who chose that year to go to the University of Texas at Austin. The quality of education I might receive there never entered my mind. I liked Austin because it was an exotic place, where students rolled about on skateboards and wore surfer shirts and water buffalo sandals; and I quickly adopted the smug view that Austin, with its "cultural aspects," was not really Texas at all. The lesson I failed to grasp, of course, was that it *was* Texas, and that I had not really wanted out of the state as much as I wanted to believe.

THAT WAS YEARS AND YEARS AGO, AND IN ALL THE time since, I have never made a conscious decision that Texas was where I was to be. Texas always seemed right for the moment, and the moments grew longer and longer, and here I remained.

Now I was beginning to feel that those years of daw-
dling and indecision amounted to a subconscious in-
vestment, that I had built up without meaning to a
certain equity of place. That was one reason why the
Massachusetts epiphany was so unwelcome.

I reacted to this crisis in a typically Texan way. I
flew to Amarillo, rented a car, and took off driving. I
had no plan really, just the raw desire to get out on the
highway system and immerse myself in Texas. There
were a few old haunts I wanted to see again and a few
places I wanted to visit for the first time, but for the
trip itself there was no excuse other than a self-
prescribed saturation therapy. I was ready for the up
cycle, ready to believe in Texas again, but I wasn't
counting on that to happen. I had a vague apprehen-
sion that in some way I was laying it all on the line,
that if Texas didn't "take" with me on this trip the clear
inference would be that I really didn't belong here
at all.

When my plane landed in Amarillo the man in the
seat next to me nodded toward the window and said,
"Pretty, isn't it?"

I'm afraid I gave him a rather blank look, because all
I saw through the same window was a vast field of concrete and, far in the distance, the hazy Amarillo sky-
line, which at first I took to be a cluster of grain
elevators.

"The weather, I mean," the man said, sheepishly.
"The *weather* is pretty."

And the weather was pretty; it was a cool, capri-
cious spring day, and every time the sun broke free

from the ragged, thin clouds it seemed to deliberately spotlight some subtle facet of that monotonous land: the geometrical pattern of the crops, the sight of black cattle against a field of frost-white native grass, the occasional swales in the landscape that were no more significant than the furrows between rows of wheat, but toward which the eye gravitated hungrily for relief from the flatness.

At a McDonald's in Amarillo I noticed a framed poster on the wall that told the story of the creation of the High Plains. God had been working on the Panhandle one day when it got dark and He had to quit. "In the morning," He said, "I'll come back and make it pretty like the rest of the world, with lakes and streams and mountains and trees."

God came back the next morning and discovered that the land had "hardened like concrete overnight." Not wanting to start all over again, He had an idea. "I know what I'll do," He said. "I'll just make some people who like it this way."

It surprised me how kindly disposed I was to this country. It was good land to drive through, though I could see what a nightmare it must have been to Coronado, day after trackless day in an unbroken field of nothingness. He and his men found some relief in Palo Duro Canyon, which to a traveler in that region is a startling rift in the plains, an opening into another dimension.

I drove through the canyon and was impressed but not overwhelmed. Texas scenery is spectacular only to Texans. Palo Duro pales beside the Grand Canyon, as the mountains of the Trans-Pecos pale beside the

Rockies, as the coasts of Texas, its forests, deserts, hills, and even its cities, seem minor variations of grander and more definitive things in other parts of the country. Texas is a zone in which the stunning vistas more or less peter out, leaving us with only one great geographical distinction: size. The prudent and prideful Texan takes in the whole package while retaining an affection for the few component parts with the necessary spit and polish to be thought of as scenery. He develops an eye for breadth, along with an ability to look close and hard at the unlovely places and graciously accept them for what they are.

So I drove out of Palo Duro with a chauvinistic fondness for the place and kept heading south through the plains. Over the stripped cotton fields the dust rose almost vertically, and the wind riled the surface of the shallow, haphazard ponds that lay by the side of the road waiting to evaporate.

Soon the land gave way a little, and there was a miniature canyon where the Floydada Country Club golf course could be seen as a brilliant green strip beneath the eroded skirts of the mesas. After that, things were flat again for a while until the Cap Rock, where the ground buckled and broke all at once. Raptors suddenly appeared, patrolling the precipice. The change in the landscape was extreme and definite. Below the Cap Rock there were scraggly, alluring vistas, adorned with the supersaturated greenery of cedar and mesquite. That late in the season there were still beds of wildflowers, and soft, thick grass cushioned the banks of the minute creeks all the way to the waterline.

I drove through Matador, Glenn, Spur, Clairmont, and only then realized that I would be driving through Snyder, where my wife's parents lived. I came into town on State Highway 208 and passed through the town square with its windowless courthouse and its fiberglass replica of the white buffalo that had been killed near there in 1876. The buffalo was Snyder's totem, and though a drunken oil-field worker might occasionally knock a hole in the statue's head with a pipe wrench, most of the people I knew looked upon it with civic reverence.

It was dinner time when I arrived at my in-laws' house, and it went without saying that we would all go out to eat a big steak.

"How about if I order for you?" my father-in-law said.

"Fine."

"Bring him the Winchester. And we want an order of fried shrimp for an appetizer."

I ate three of these shrimp, each nearly the size of a potato, before the Winchester arrived. It was a big slab of beef, but I was hungry from driving and correctly calculated that I could put it away.

While we ate, my father-in-law complained with genial fervor about the state of the world. Since Reagan had been elected, he did not have quite so much to gripe about anymore. But even so, he had a few things on his mind. He was mad because the Democratic Congress wouldn't let the Republicans take a measly billion dollars from the synthetic fuel fund to stimulate the housing industry; mad because the British and the Argentineans were going to have a war over the Falkland Islands and guess who was going to have to go in there after it was all over with billions of dollars of foreign aid; mad because he had casually returned his YES token to the *Reader's Digest* sweepstakes and now he was being deluged with junk mail.

"There's something you should write an article about for your *Texas Monthly*," he said as we pulled out of the driveway of the restaurant, indicating a long-bodied motor home parked next to us. "These vans or whatever they are that block your view of the street when you're trying to pull out."

All of this good-natured grumpiness made me feel at home, and I lingered into the evening and finally ended up walking across the street to the high school with my mother-in-law to watch the production of *Ah, Wilderness!* that had recently won the state one-act-play competition. I was glad to have an excuse to see the high school where my wife had been a student, where she had edited the paper and written a column, under the name of Sonya Stifled, complaining about the Vietnam War and the lack of paper straws in the cafeteria.

The production took place in an immense auditorium that had been built with tax money from the great fifties oil boom. The play itself was minor O'Neill but showed Snyder High School's drama department to superlative advantage. One or two of the actors even managed very creditable New England accents. When the play was over and the audience was strolling out into the spring night, Snyder appeared less like a West Texas oil town than the idyllic Connecticut village that had been depicted in the play, a place with a tight matrix of tradition and community. It did not seem like the stifling place my wife had written about years ago, the place I might have glanced at contemptuously from the highway as I barreled through on my way to some hippie mecca in New Mexico. It seemed alarmingly like home.

THE NEXT DAY I GOT ON INTERSTATE 20 AND DROVE to Abilene, finding by dead reckoning the house we had lived in more than twenty years earlier. The owners had painted it yellow and put a ceramic burro in the yard, and the neighborhood itself was largely shaded from the searing sun I had known there by all the trees that had grown up and over it in the last two decades.

It was all so comfortable and congenial: the creeks were swollen with bright ocher water, the streets were lined with upscale shops and the great Danish modern cathedrals of the Protestant faith, and the movie theaters were showing *Deathtrap* and *Conan the Barbarian*. I wondered if I was feeling warm toward Texas again because it was more acceptable than I had thought or simply because it was familiar.

The land between Abilene and Dallas was unremarkable, but it held the attention of the practiced eye. In another month it would lose its verdant sheen; it would be dry and scruffy, and the very contours of the landscape would appear to recede and lose definition. But I had a fondness for that too, tucked away somewhere.

In this accepting mood I surged through Dallas in the shadow of the Reunion Tower, which had always looked to me like the centerpiece to a bush league world's fair. But there was no city in the country that was honed to such a fine edge as Dallas, and you could sense its organic singleness of purpose, its obsession to project style and busyness. You were either on the team or not.

I was on the team that day, and I drove confidently through the streets, enjoying the familiar feel of the city. Then I headed south on I-35, going through Waco and Temple and past a wacky entrepreneurial jumble on the side of the highway that included a crumbling replica of the Matterhorn. Then on U.S. 183 to Lockhart, where I arrived in time to witness a reenactment of the Battle of Plum Creek. Bleachers were set up on the battlefield, microphones were planted into the ground. This epic, with its meager cast of dozens, required some thrifty stage management. A Texas Ranger would ride in on a horse and announce, "I been shot by one of them dad-blamed Indians," and his mount would then be led off the stage, shuttled around behind the bleachers, and ridden in from the other side by a Comanche with a beer gut.

The pageant served less to bring the past to life than to make the present seem anemic and unreal. But Plum Creek itself, several miles away, had not been milked of its drama. It was Edenic, and along with every other creek I passed that day on my meandering way south—La Parra, Agua Dulce, Papalote—it had a lush, overgrown, hummocky quality that made you understand why this part of the country had been the fertile crescent of Texas history.

Even farther south, in the brush country of Jim

Wells and Duval counties, the land was surprisingly green, so much so that the dilapidated, boarded-up main streets of the less successful towns looked as if they were in danger of being reclaimed by jungle. Swallows dipped ahead of my car in relays, and turkey vultures and caracaras fed together on dead baby armadillos that had been struck down on the highway in their earliest forays.

A friend's father was being buried in San Diego that day, and I had adjusted my itinerary so that I would pass through town in time to attend the funeral. The church stood across the street from a zocalo whose gazebo and benches had been overgrown with grass and whose function as the center of town had been usurped by the highway a block away. Inside, the church was stolid and secure, its walls painted a light blue. Beside the altar was a full-color pietà, with dark red blood trickling from Christ's wounds and Mary bent down on one knee, holding her son's body in a way that suggested both sorrow and verve. It was a fine, grisly statue, with that admirable Mexican trait of being on square terms with mortal matters, a trait that was not echoed in the liturgically trendy stained glass windows bearing happy cubist depictions of doves and chalices and unsplintered crosses.

The congregation was dressed in suits and pressed ranch clothes. The service moved along in an unflinching manner, its bone-deep rituals making death seem real but not necessarily final.

I got back into my car feeling sobered and transient, a little flicker of movement on the landscape. But soon enough my attention was drawn outward again. The country was full of arresting things, from the painted bunting I saw preening its iridescent body in a mud puddle in Swinney Switch to a herd of Brahman bulls that had gathered at dusk near the gate of a fence outside Floresville. In that light the bulls' hides were the color of marble; their pendulous scrotums swayed above the rich grass, and their curious humps twitched when they shifted their weight from one hoof to another. At the gate stood a man in a red cap. He was not doing anything, just standing there with the bulls, and they in turn seemed thoughtlessly drawn to him.

It began to grow dark, in a peaceful, sodden way, as if the air were absorbing darkness rather than relinquishing light. The radio said that the widow of Pancho Villa had died, but then the station disappeared in a flurry of static before I could hear details. I tuned in an ad for Diamond Head water troughs, followed by a self-conscious country song in which Hank Williams, Jr., managed to drop the names of Willie and Waylon and Kris in lamenting the sad fact that nobody wanted to go out and get drunk with him anymore. The night deepened and the voices on the radio grew more desperate:

> You got to look that devil in the eye if you're sufferin' from satanic oppression. You got to say, "Devil, in the name of Jesus of Nazareth, take your hands offa my *finances*!"

> And Bob?
> Yessir.
> I just wanted to say something about this El Salvadorian business.

Sorry. We're about out of time.

I don't see why we just can't take one of them tactical nuclear bombs . . .

Gotta go.

Now, wait a minute. Put that bomb in downtown Nicaragua or wherever . . .

Bye . . .

I COASTED HOME TO AUSTIN ON THE STRAINS OF A song about a honky-tonk cowboy who was doomed to a life of loneliness because he couldn't dance the cotton-eyed Joe. I went to bed feeling glum and perplexed, having expected that by now all those images and impressions of Texas would have formed themselves into a single testament. But I was still at arm's length, still mildly estranged. I just couldn't dance the cotton-eyed Joe.

IN THE MORNING MY FIVE-YEAR-OLD DAUGHTER was whiny and irritable when I took her to school, and after pacing around the house for a while in more or less the same mood I drove back to the school to pick her up.

"Where are we going?" she asked. "To the dentist?"

"No. To Enchanted Rock."

"What's that?"

"It's a special place."

"Oh. Like Disneyland."

We listened to her Little Thinker tape as we drove west through the LBJ country, where the roadside peach vendors were just putting up their stalls, and on through Fredericksburg, with its Sunday houses and German bakeries and relentless old-country quaintness.

The first we saw of Enchanted Rock was a bare salmon-colored nubbin erupting from the serene Hill Country vista ahead. The nubbin quickly loomed larger, until it was clearly a great stone mountain, so huge and abruptly *there* that all perspective dropped away and the rock had the one-dimensional clarity of a scene that has been painted on a panel of glass.

I felt an impatience to be there, to climb to the top. Enchanted Rock was perhaps my favorite Texas place, an immense granite batholith that the Indians had considered sacred. I had found it to be sacred too, and it was to Enchanted Rock that I used to come when I was in an especially powerful sulking mood.

We came quickly to the base of the rock, and above us, as we got out of the car, we could see the deep crease across its brow along which several minute figures crept upward.

"Wow," said my daughter. "Are we going to climb that?"

We were. We jumped across the half-dozen or so separate threads of water that composed Big Sandy Creek and followed the trail upward until it was lost in the expanse of solid rock. Then we walked up at a sharp angle, stopping about every fifteen yards so my daughter could rest and express disbelief at how far we had come. Near the top, where it was very steep, she got a little testy, so I picked her up and carried her to the summit.

"Boy," she said, as I staggered along with her in my arms, "mountain climbing is hard, isn't it?"

Finally I set her down next to a plaque that had been riveted into the rock.

"What does it say?"

"It says, 'Enchanted Rock. From its summit in the fall of 1841, Captain John C. Hays, while surrounded by Comanche Indians who cut him off from his ranging company, repulsed the whole band and inflicted upon them such heavy losses that they fled.' "

"What does that mean?"

"It means a guy had a fight with Indians up here."

"But Indians are nice now, aren't they? They only use their bows and arrows for practice."

Yes, Indians were nice now. Texas itself was nice, no longer a hostile country battled over by contentious spirits, but a reasonably representative American place, filled with familiar and ephemeral things: Wal-Marts, civic ballets, wind surfing, cable TV, Hare Krishnas in business suits. But Texas had not been wholly digested somehow, and in places like Enchanted Rock you could still get a buzz, you could still feel its insistent identity.

From the top the rock was as barren as the moon, and its vast surface canted forward slightly, so that there were two horizons, the rim of the mountain and, beyond it, the edge of the true world. I hoped this sight would take with my daughter; when her sisters were older I would bring them up here too so that Enchanted Rock could seep into their memories. I felt this place belonged to them, more than to me; they were native Texans, after all.

The lag, the missed beat I felt in my relationship with Texas, was something that I trusted would be corrected in future generations. And for the present, Enchanted Rock was every bit as much a power cen-

ter for me as that sandstone boulder back in Oklahoma City. And there were others: a certain stretch of
the Frio River, where after weeks of senseless brood-
ing I had made up my mind to go ahead and be happy
and get married; the lobby of the Menger hotel in San
Antonio, where there was a plaque dedicated to the
memory of Sidney Lanier and where you could find a
gigantic Titianesque Nativity scene hung near a paint-
ing titled *Venting Cattle on the Frisco Range;* the Indian
pictographs in Seminole Canyon; the mud flats and
back bays of Laguna Madre; the old Shanghai Jimmy's
Chili Rice on Lemmon Avenue in Dallas, where you
were served chili by the man who claimed he had
introduced that dish to China during the Boxer Re-
bellion; the Chinati Mountains; the Flower Gardens
coral reef; the thick, suffocating Big Thicket forests,
where you could find quicksand and wild orchids; any
number of places that would give you all the barbecue
you could eat for $7 or $8, where you could sit beneath a pressed-tin ceiling on a humid midsummer
evening, give the baby a rib bone to gnaw on to help
her with her teething, and pursue the illusion that life
outside Texas would be bland and charmless. Texas
for me was a thousand things like that, a thousand
moments that in my mind had been charged with a
special quality of place that I could not explain or
understand. I only knew that the quality, and the
place, was Texas.

A fault line ran across the back of Enchanted Rock
like the stitching on a baseball. There was a sort of
cave there, illuminated by the gaps between the collapsed boulders that had formed it, where we went to

drink our apple juice. My daughter announced she wanted to play Indian.

"You be the daddy Indian," she said. "You can be taking a nap while I make the tea."

I closed my eyes obediently and felt the cool air of the cave on my face. I let the whole Texas question rest. "I'll just make some people who like it this way," God had said. I wasn't sure if I had been put on the earth with an inborn love for Texas, but I certainly seemed to have a high tolerance for it. Lying there in the cave, on the summit of an ancient and hallowed mountain, I still felt a mild longing to live someplace that was more exotic, or more ordinary; someplace that was not Texas. One of these days I might do that. Just not today.